# NewMusicShelf

# Anthology of New Music
## Soprano, Vol. 1

Curated by Laura Strickling
Edited by Dennis Tobenski

Foreword by Libby Larsen

**NewMusicShelf**
www.newmusicshelf.com

NEWMUSICSHELF, INC.

Published in the United States of America
by NewMusicShelf, Inc.
34-29 32nd St., 3rd floor, Astoria, NY 11106
www.newmusicshelf.com

Copyright © 2018 by NewMusicShelf, Inc.

First printing 2018

All rights reserved. No part of this publication may be reproduced, stored in a retrieval system, or transmitted in any form or by any means, electronic, mechanical, photocopying, recording, or otherwise, without the prior permission of the publisher.

*to everyone on #teamartsong*

# Contents

Acknowledgments .................................................................................... vii
Foreword by Libby Larsen ......................................................................... ix
Editor's Preface ........................................................................................ x
Introduction ............................................................................................ xi

**John Arrigo-Nelson:** Grapheme I after Cy Twombly (2017) ............................. 1

**Paul Ayres:** The Best-Beloved (2005) ........................................................ 15

**Clint Borzoni:** Oh You Whom I Often and Silently Come (2010) .................... 24

**Mark Buller:** Mr. Peck (2015) .................................................................. 32
   *from* The Tombstone Songs

**Martin Bussey:** Lovely Playthings (2005) .................................................. 37
   *from* Three Gurney Songs

**Emerson Eads:** He Wishes for the Cloths of Heaven (2013) ........................... 41

**Evan Fein:** Lullaby for a Baby Fairy (2011) ............................................... 46

**Daniel Felsenfeld:** Dry Sandwiches (2007) ................................................ 51

**Jodi Goble:** The Storm (2016) ................................................................. 61
   *from* The Heart of the World

**Juliana Hall:** Song (1987) ...................................................................... 66
   *from* Night Dances

**Gordon Kerry:** Canto of the Leaves (Empyrean) (2009) ................................ 71
   *from* Five Cantos from 'Divine Comedy:
       Journeys through a Regional Geography'

**Joshua Lindsay:** Fall, Leaves, Fall (2017) .................................................. 80

**Cecilia Livingston:** Penelope (2014) .................................................. 85

**Raymond J. Lustig:** the silvery round moon (2008) .................................................. 98

**Carrie Magin:** Be Music, Night (2011) .................................................. 106

**James Matheson:** Clouds ripped open (2012) .................................................. 115
    *from* Times Alone

**James Primosch:** Every Day is a God (2012) .................................................. 124
    *from* Holy the Firm

**Behzad Ranjbaran:** It Is Night (1987) .................................................. 143
    *from* Three Persian Songs

**William Toutant:** Le Pont Mirabeau (2015) .................................................. 149

**Theodore Wiprud:** Elegy Before Death (2010) .................................................. 157
    *from* For Allegra

About the Curator .................................................. 163
About the Composers .................................................. 164
Supplemental Materials .................................................. 184

# Foreword

Congratulations! You hold in your hands the *NewMusicShelf Anthologies of New Music*, a four-volume, curated treasure trove of 80 songs penned by your colleague composers and composed for you, singer of songs, teller of tales, bearer of our zeitgeist. Discover and prize these songs. They are yours now, in your keeping, waiting to rise on your breath and sing through your voices.

You might think of these four volumes of song as living-history - a vibrant mix of singers, collaborative instrumentalists, composers and our audiences. A wide range of the many excellent composers writing art song today are represented here. They are a community of composers who love the human voice and devote their talent and time to composing new work for it. We honor these composers through performance, of course, by singing the songs they write for us. We also must remind ourselves that we need to honor their work by respecting their need to support themselves with compensation in the form of the royalties they collect from sales of their music. We urge you to support your composers by resisting the temptation to photocopy and distribute music from these song collections. As the world becomes more and more digital, we think it essential that these collections of songs are available only in print. In the years to come we will be delighted to discover the *NewMusicShelf Anthologies of New Music* on pianos, bookshelves and music stands, but even more delighted to hear you filling the air with the sound of your singing - these songs - everywhere!

— Libby Larsen

# Acknowledgments

My deepest thanks to…

The composers who have inspired me by their dedication to the written word and to the vast possibilities of the human voice.

Dennis Tobenski, for giving me to the opportunity to immerse myself in the worlds of hundreds of songs.

The teachers who helped me find my voice: George Rico, Susan Clark Manns, William Sharp, Phyllis Bryn-Julson, and Elizabeth Daniels.

The pianists who have joined me in exploring the vast world of song: Joy Schreier, Liza Stepanova, Daniel Schlosberg, Michael Brofman, Miori Sugiyama, Brent Funderburk, Dimitri Dover, Spencer Myer, Xak Bjerken.

The woman who, in my opinion, has made the most lasting impact on the singing of songs in the United States, the founder of Songfest, Rosemary Hyler Ritter.

The singer whose commitment to song repertoire and supporting the community of singers of songs has served as a model and encouragement to me, Paul Sperry.

My husband, Taylor, who has - in every tangible and intangible way - supported my journey of Being a Singer.

The most beautiful song I've ever sung, my daughter Elizabeth.

— Laura Strickling

# Editor's Preface

This volume - and series of publications - exists to introduce performing musicians to the amazing variety of composers living and writing today. Whether you're a student, teacher, or professional, this collection was created with you in mind.

Every song is appropriate for a professional or student recital, and many songs were selected for their didactic possibilities: shifting meters, asymmetrical rhythms, various degrees of difficulty with pitch materials or non-traditional performance techniques, etc.

Across all four inaugural volumes of these anthologies, the primary criterion has been the curator's willingness to stand behind their selections: to be willing to perform and record every song, and make their selections without reservation. These are songs that singers should *know*, and should perform. These are composers that singers should *know*, and should work with.

And *you* are performers that composers should get to know and work with! We are all a part of a community that makes music, and we can only be better and stronger together.

As the creator of this series, I've had to personally define my short-, medium-, and long-term goals for the project. My short-term goal is simple: you getting to know these songs, and performing them. I stand behind every song and every composer, and hope that you find your own connection to these songs.

My medium-term goal is linked to a minor feature of these volumes: notice that underneath many of the song titles there is a bit of text: "from _____". Many of these songs are from song cycles or song sets. I encourage you to check out those cycles, as well as the composer's other vocal works! My medium-term goal? That you and your colleagues get to know more of the works by these composers than are represented here. This is a mere sliver of these composers' output, and their catalogs are worth exploring!

My long-term goal? Let's just say that I have plans....

I encourage you to look beyond the borders of the voice-type specific nature of these volumes. Many of these songs were written without gender or voice type in mind, and so are worth exploring by every singer.

— Dennis Tobenski
Founder of NewMusicShelf

# Introduction

Nothing happens in a vacuum, and it happened that the deliberation stage of the NewMusicShelf Anthology project coincided with a major event in my life. Two category five hurricanes (Irma and Maria) destroyed our US Virgin Islands community, as well as several neighboring islands, over the course of two weeks in September 2018. With an infant and no access to electricity or water, we fled our home to live with family on the mainland for the better part of 7 months.

To say that my spirit needed the nourishment of song during this time is an understatement. I listened to hundreds of song submissions and felt personally renewed little by little. What a wonderful gift these composers have – to read words and be inspired by them to create a response that binds music to them. The only agonizing part was choosing just 20 out of the hundreds of submissions, and in this I plead that these selections are my opinion and mine alone. I have no doubt that another curator would have made different choices than I did, but that is the nature of art: It is subjective and just as the composer creates in reaction to words so, too, does a performer create and become inspired by a subjective, ephemeral reaction.

I believe in the power of song. Words matter. Music matters. Song recitals provide an opportunity for a performer to create a narrative through repertoire selection. Each work transports the listener to a different place, a different time, a different way to look at the world around them – bringing each of us closer to a deeper understanding of the human experience. I always tell audiences that they have learned things about me as a person – what interests me, what I find beautiful or exciting, what my values are – by my song selections for a recital, and so you also, holding this anthology, have learned something about me and about each of these composers. You are afforded a small window into the compositional output of 20 composers of great skill and it is my sincere hope that you will explore their other works, as well as new works of composers not represented in this anthology, working right now to build worlds of song to stand as a testament of the power of words set to music.

— Laura Strickling

# Grapheme I after Cy Twombly
## Performance Notes

**Soprano**

1. Any *diminuendo* to a rest should be to a *niente* dynamic unless otherwise indicated.

2. Microtonal accidentals (♮ ♭ etc.) do not indicate specific quarter tones, but rather a general alteration of the traditional accidental ("a slightly lowered natural", "a slightly lowered flat", etc.).

3. *Portamento* is indicated with a "*port.*" before the second note of the *portamento* figure.

4. *Glissandi* are indicated with a diagonal line between notes, and should start immediately on the note indicated and fill the entire rhythmic calue of that note.

5. The three non-singing techniques used are indicated as follows:

***Sprechstimme:*** X-noteheads with approximate pitch indication

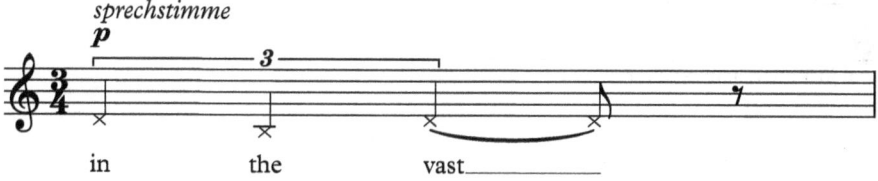

**Speaking:** X-noteheads on center line

**Half-whisper:** X-noteheads with slash through stem

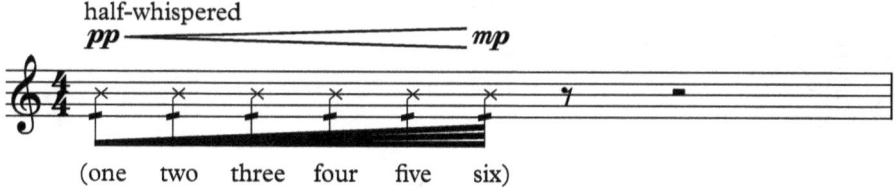

6. See piano performance note #8

**Piano**

1. A "+" applied to a note indicates to pluck the corresponding string inside the piano

2. Stem up/down with arrow: Sweep finger(s) across the strings once in the direction indicated

3. Diamond: Apply sustain pedal after a sharply-struck chord. The sound of the resonating strings partially caught by the sustain pedal is symbolized by the large diamond between the two staves. To produce the desired effect, lower pitches will require more time between the articulation of the chord and application of the pedal.

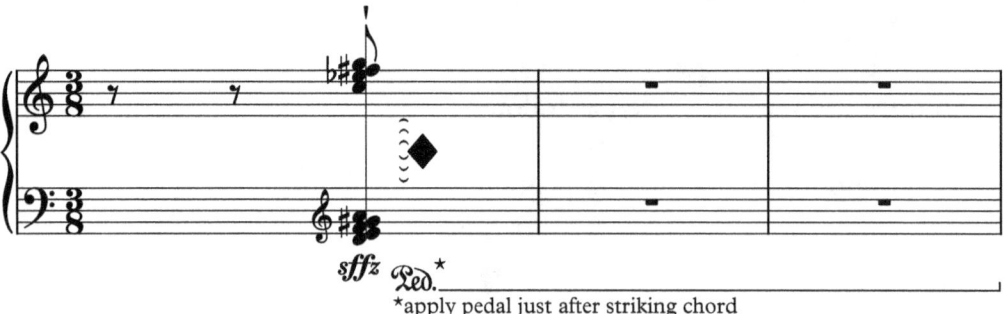

*apply pedal just after striking chord

4. Triangle noteheads indicate the range of a gesture that is to be played on the strings inside the piano. With a smooth wavy line, gently sweep the fingertip(s) back and forth continuously with no particular regard for the prevailing tempo.

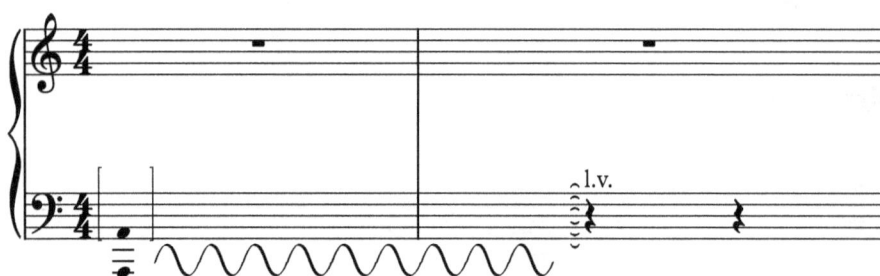

5. Triangle noteheads indicate the range of a gesture that is to be played on the strings inside the piano. With an uneven wavy line, gently sweep fingertip(s) back and forth arrythmically across the strings continually; also include occasional lightly accented articulations with the back of your fingernail.

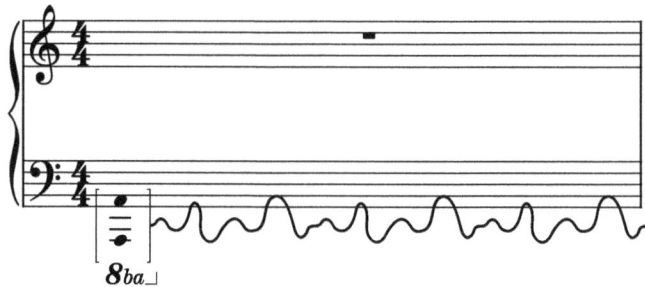

6. Harmonics: The bass clef note is to be played at the keybaord and held until the pedal is applied. The floating diamond notehead above the bass clef indicates thatt he corresponding string is to be simultaneously touched to produce the pitches indicated in bracketed small noteheads in the treble clef. (As soon as the note is played at the keyboard, the touching finger should be removed from the string.)

Other overtones may be present, but the ones indicated are obligatory and will be the most prominent. The indicated overtones in the treble clef are expressed in equal temperment; actual sounding overtones may deviate from the indicated pitches by some microtonal interval.

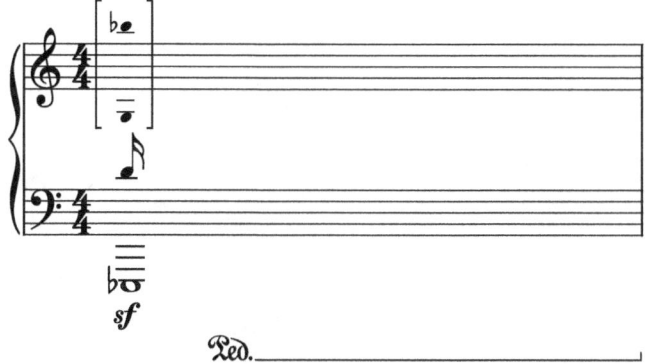

7. Within the approximate indicated range (triangle noteheads), "strum" strings inside the piano by fanning four fingers back and forth across the strings continuously, maintaining contact with the strings throughout the figure.

Strings will be articulated by fingertips/fingerpads mostly, but some fingernail articulation may be present, as well.

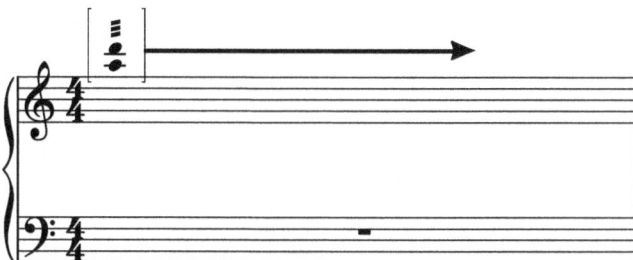

# Grapheme I after Cy Twombly

JOHN ARRIGO-NELSON
(2017)

\* grace notes should always precede the beat
\*\* ossia 8va higher

Copyright © 2017 by ArrigoMusic. All Rights Reserved.

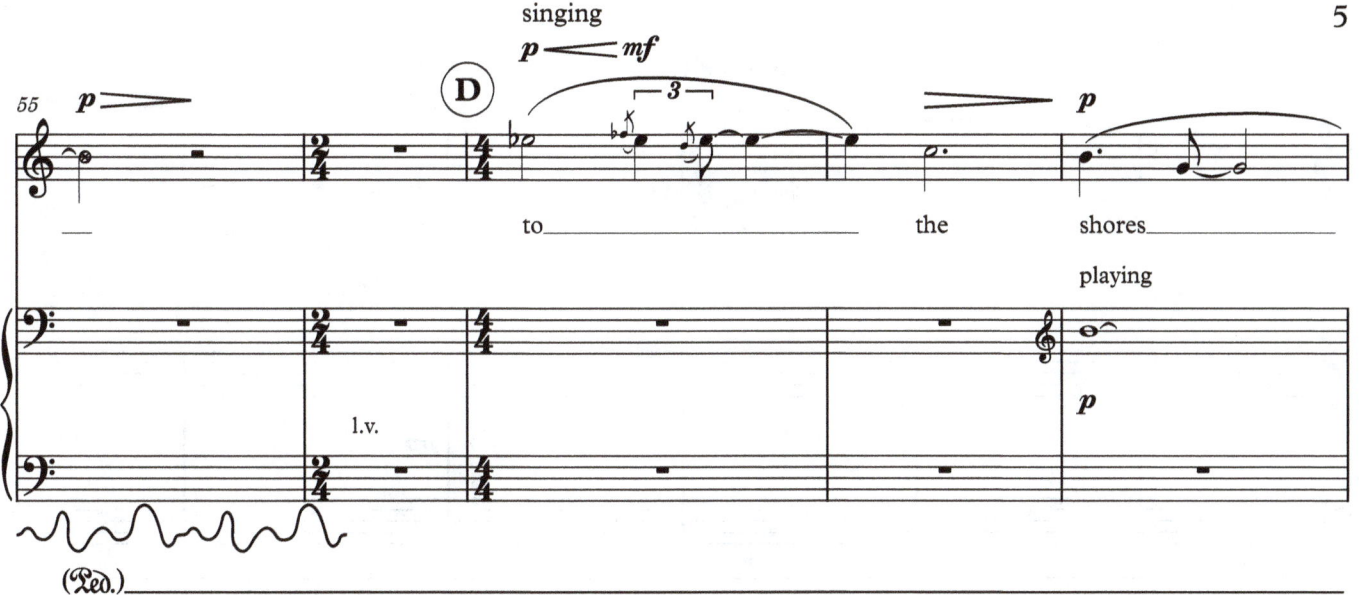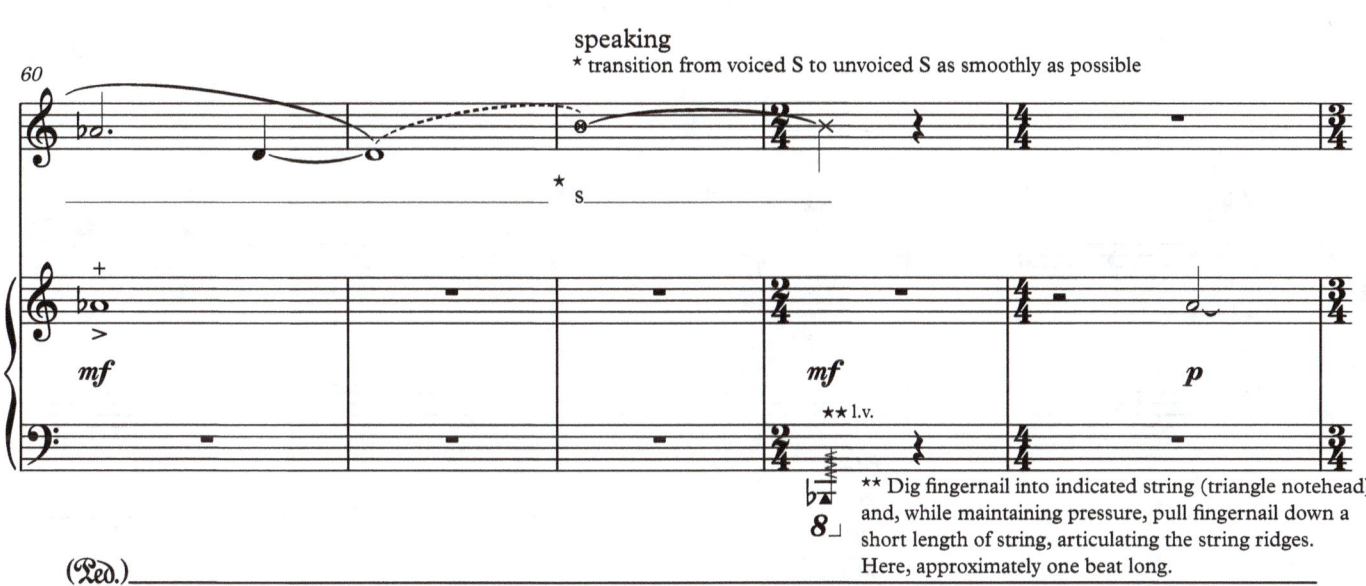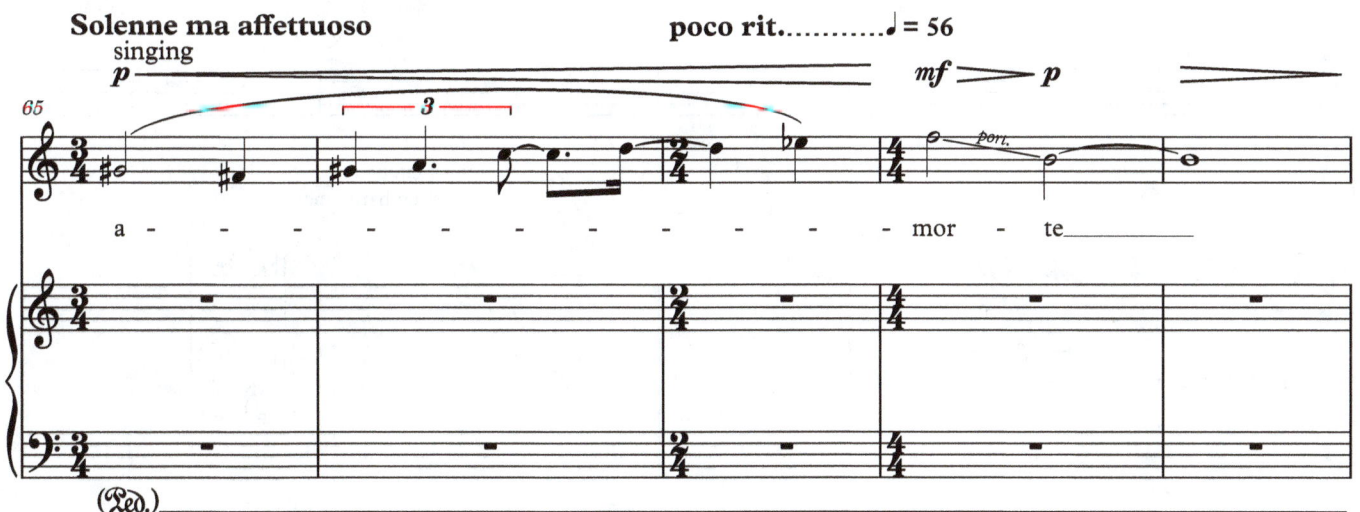

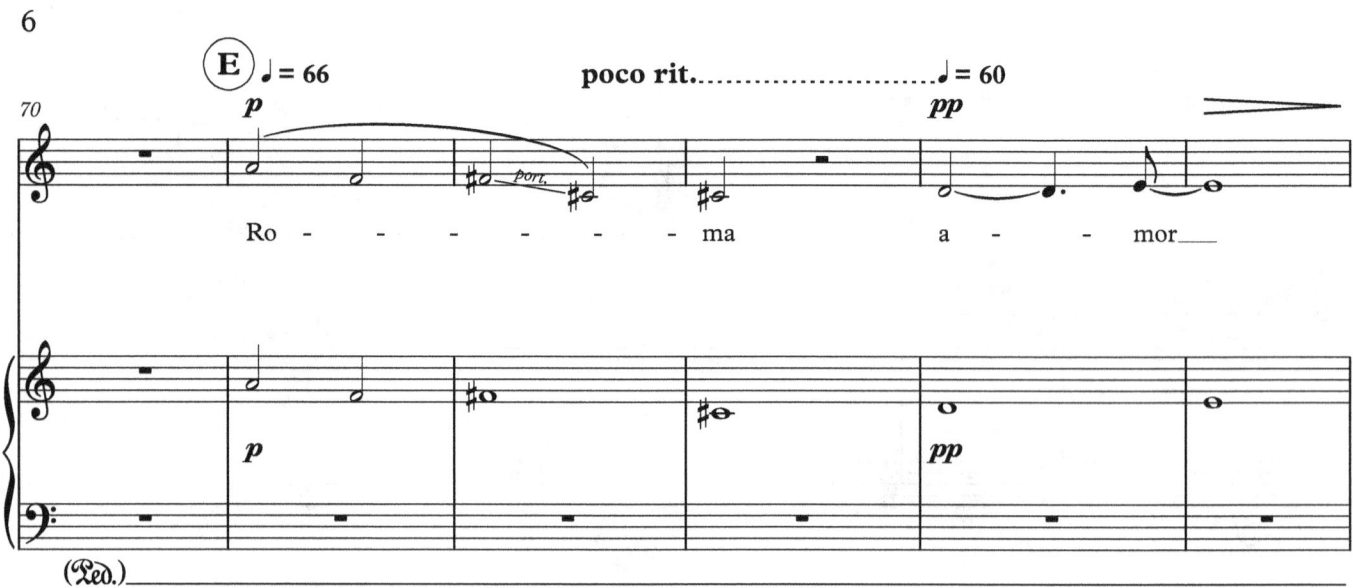
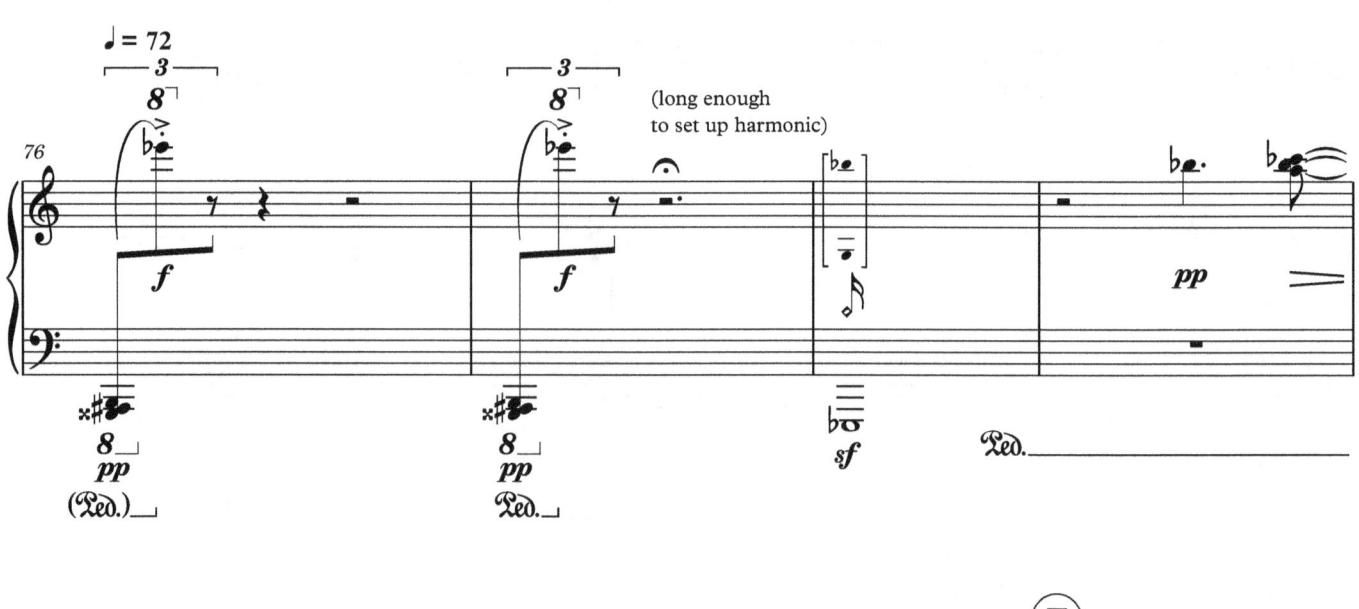
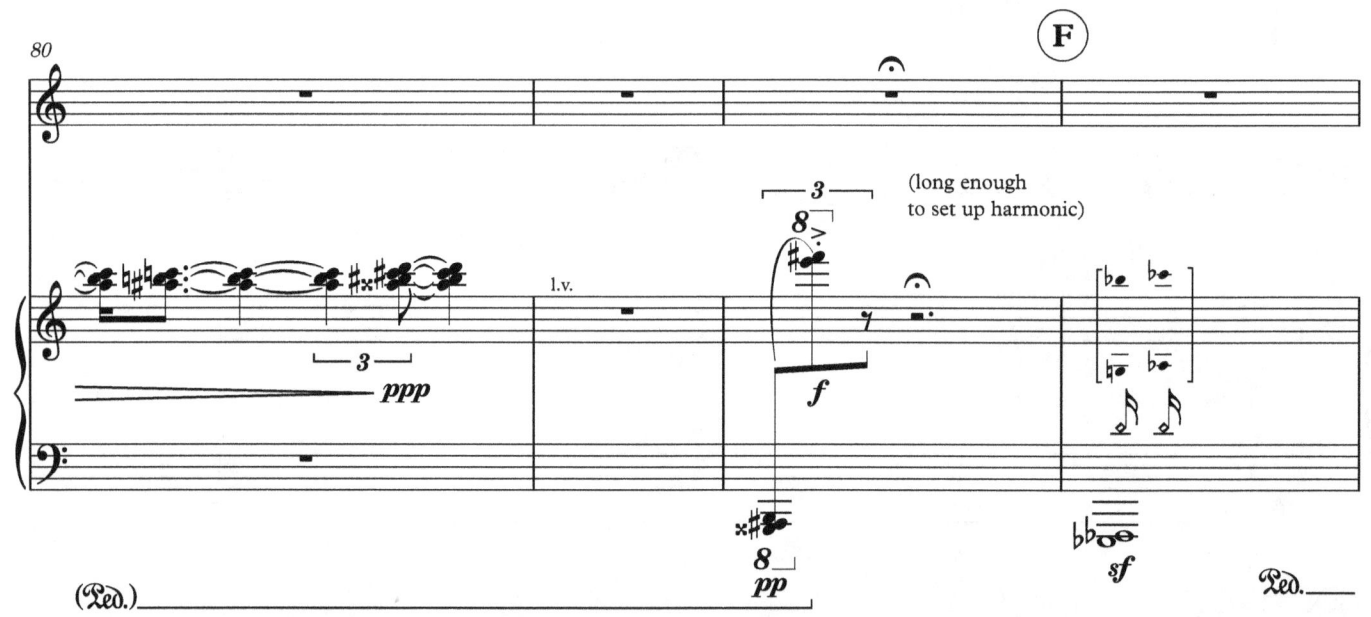

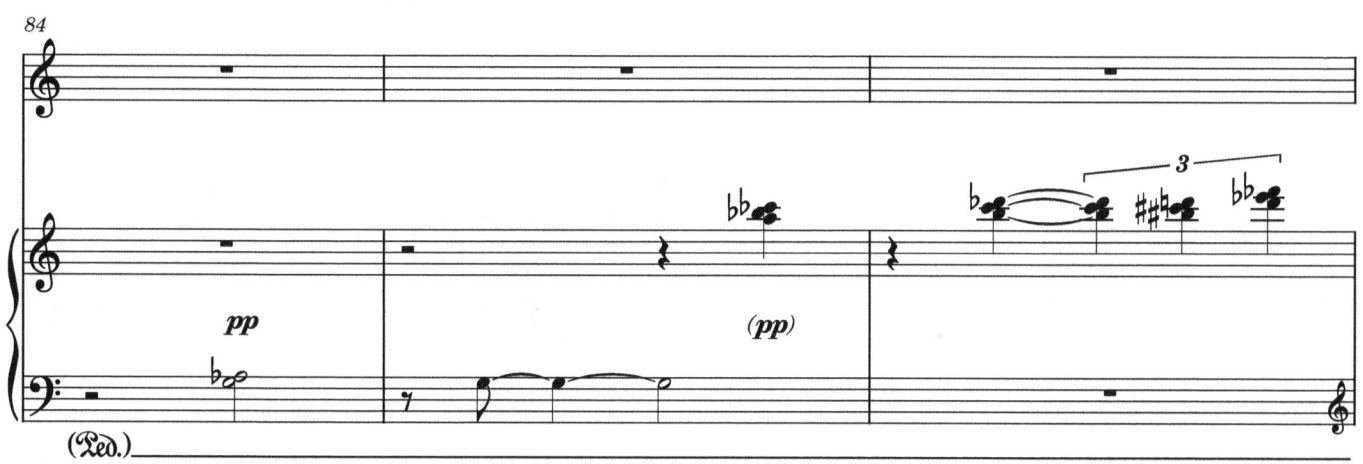
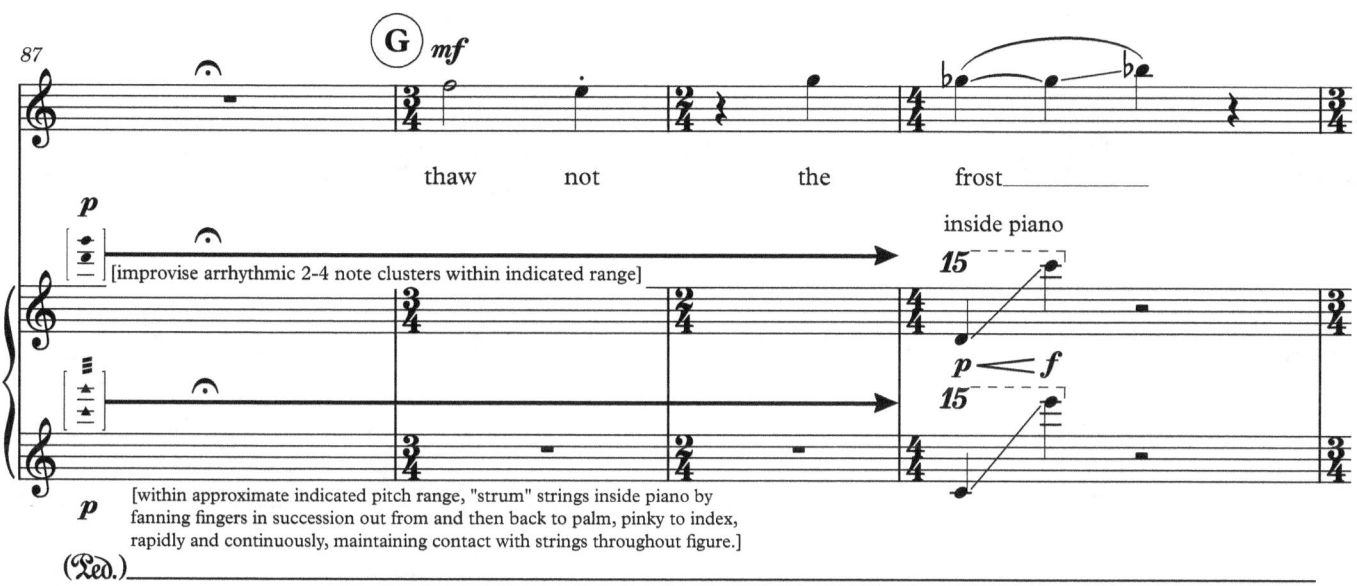
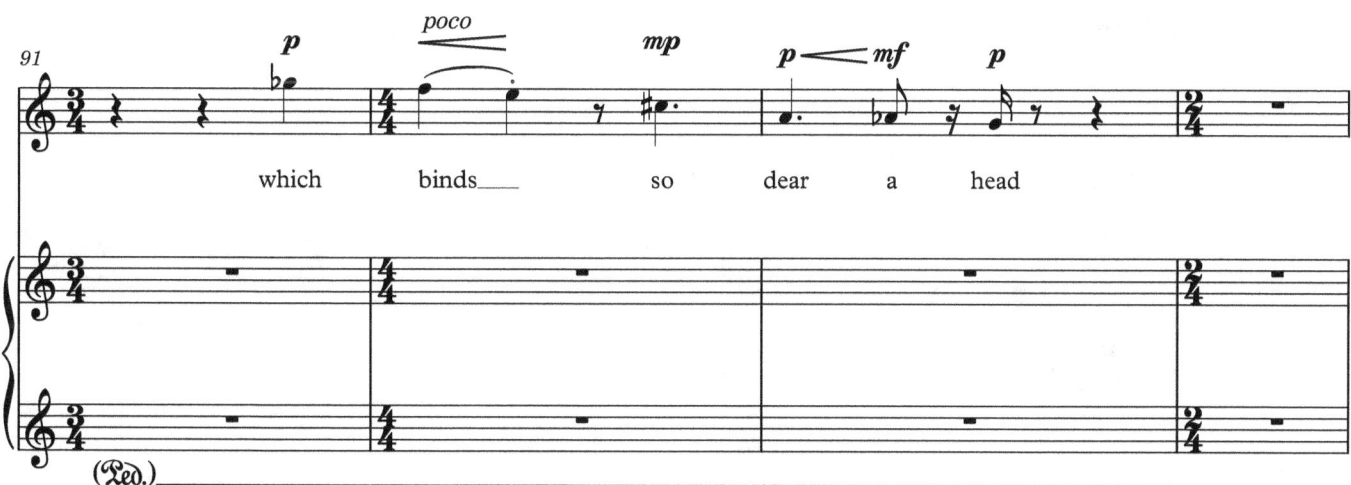

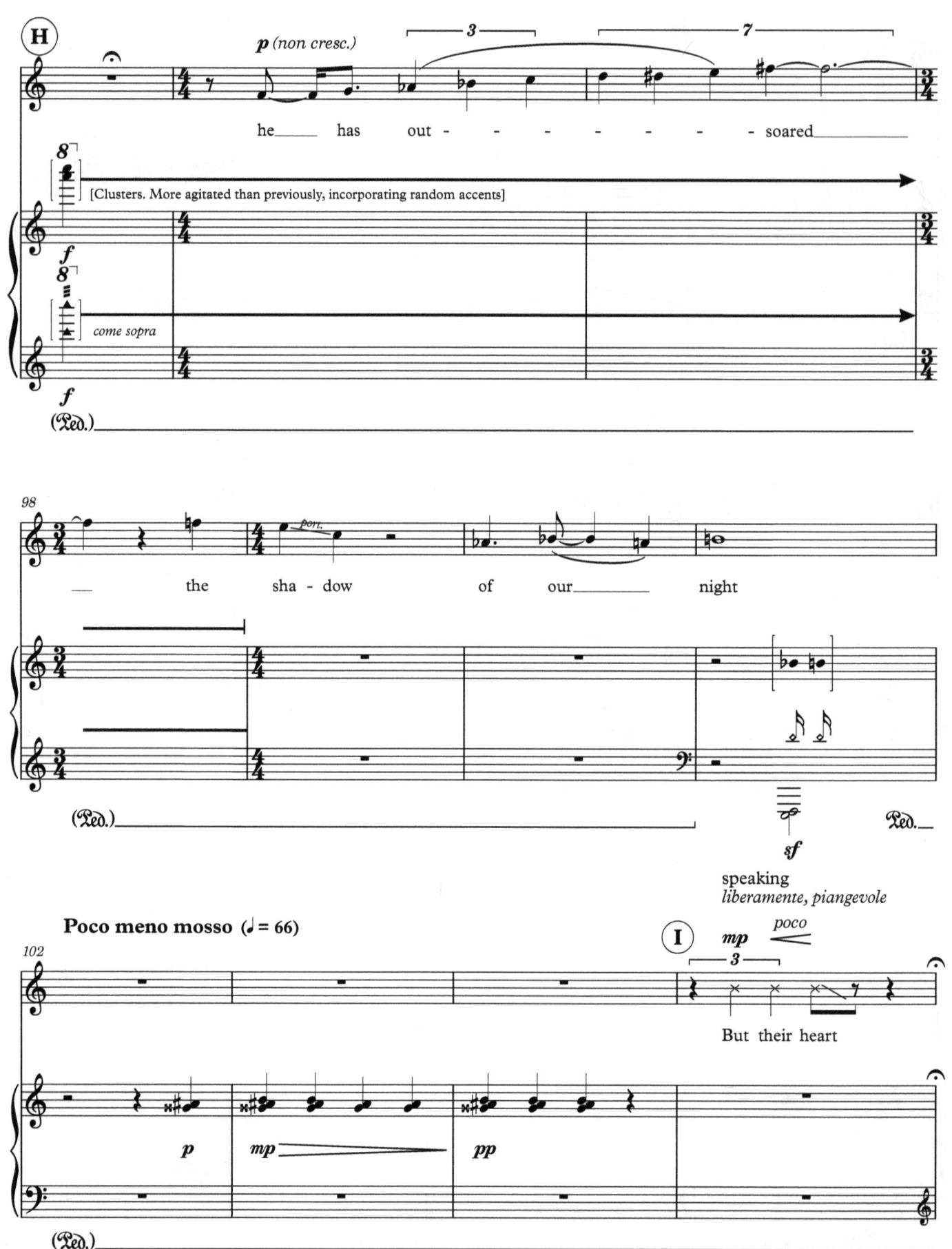

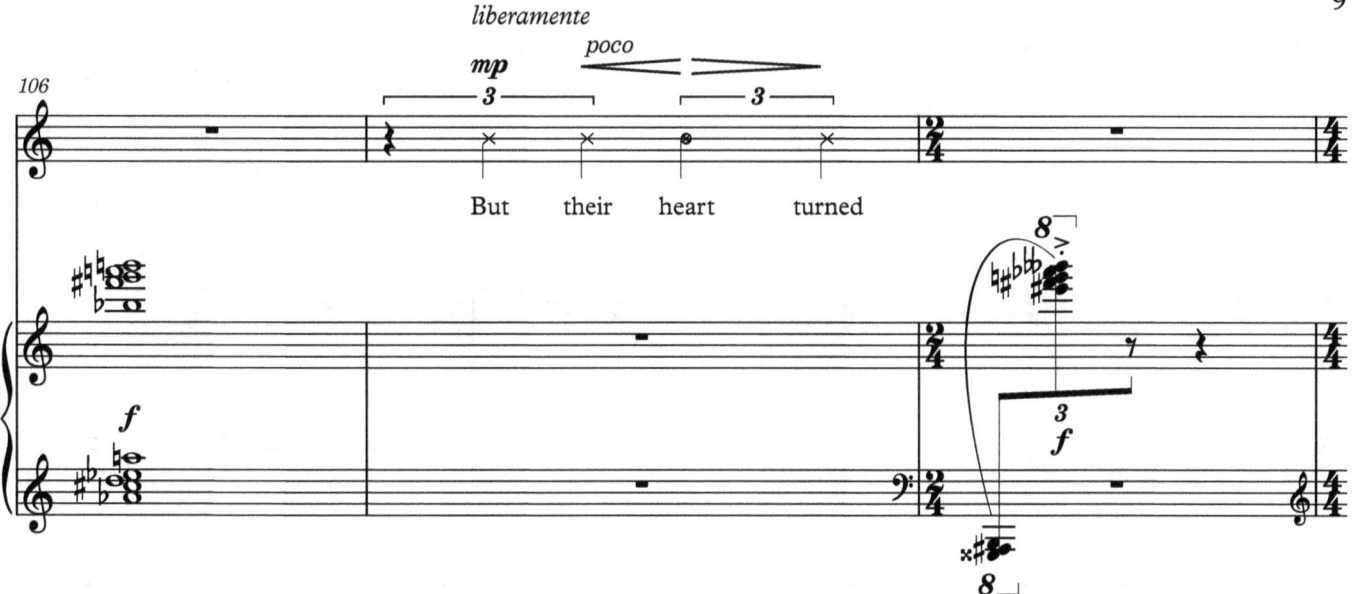
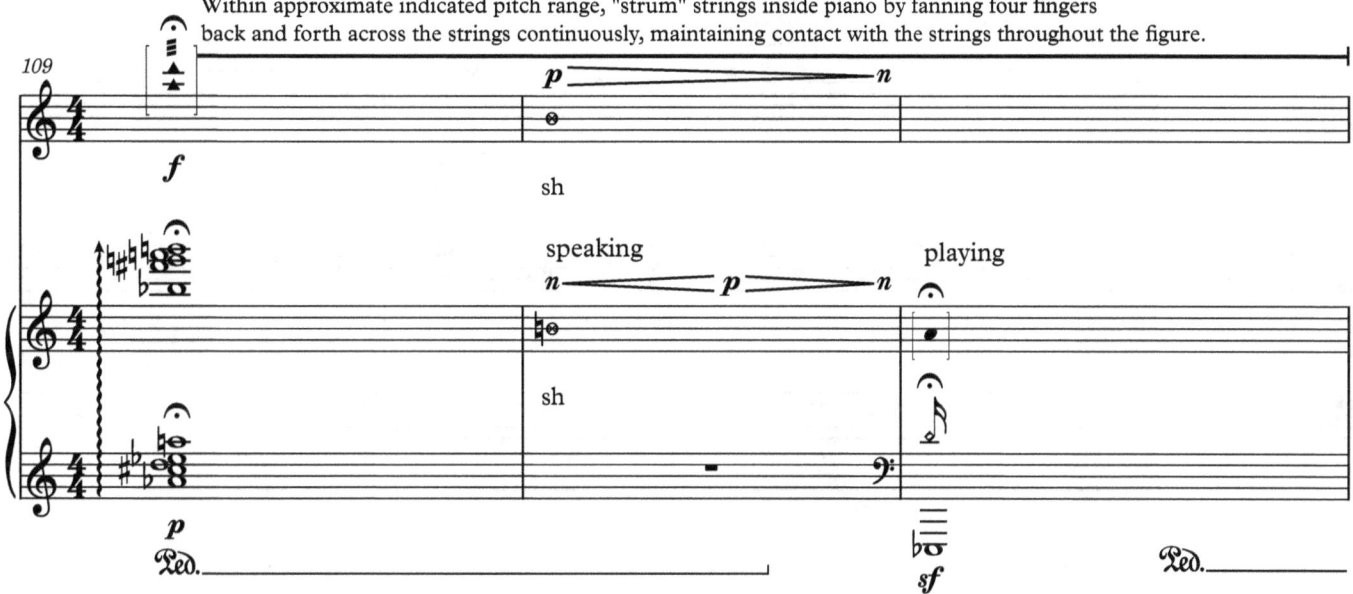
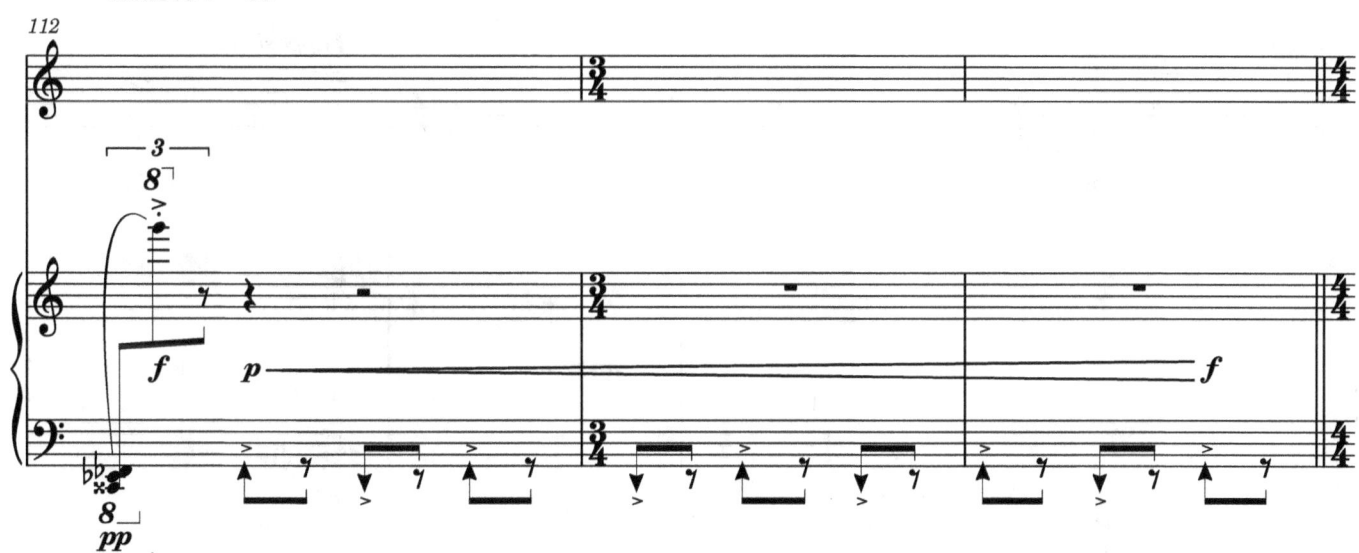

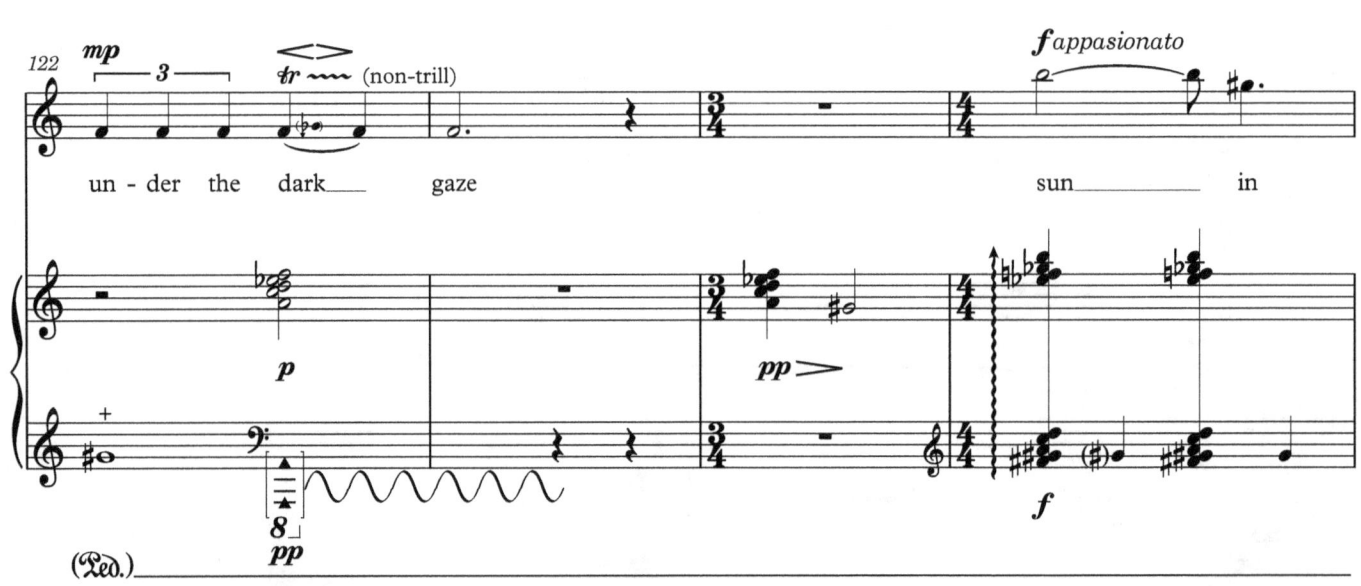

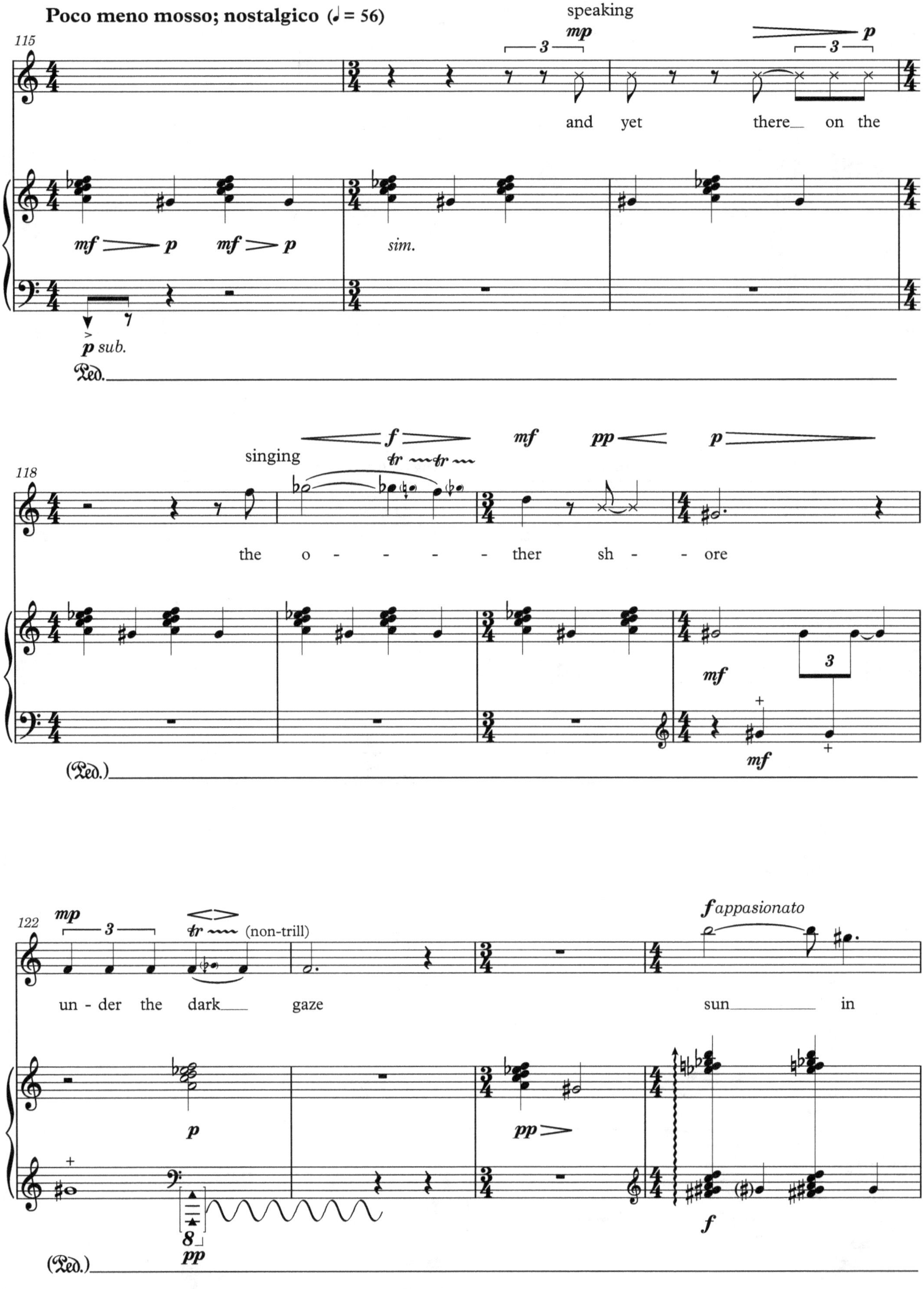
Poco meno mosso; nostalgico (♩ = 56)
speaking
and yet there on the
p sub.
Ped.
singing
the o - - - - - ther sh - - ore
(Ped.)
mp
(non-trill)
un - der the dark gaze
f appasionato
sun in
sim.

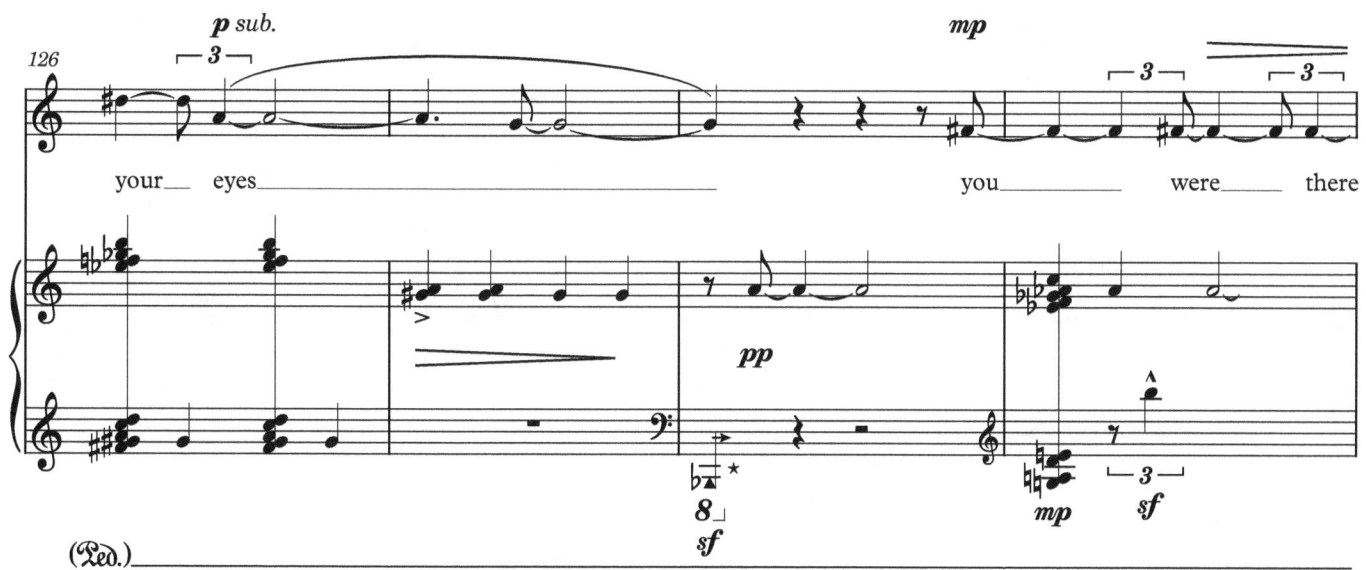

*With finger curled toward palm, dig back of fingernail into indicated string (triangle notehead), then quickly extend finger outward in a single "flicking" motion, articulating string with both fingernail and fingertip.

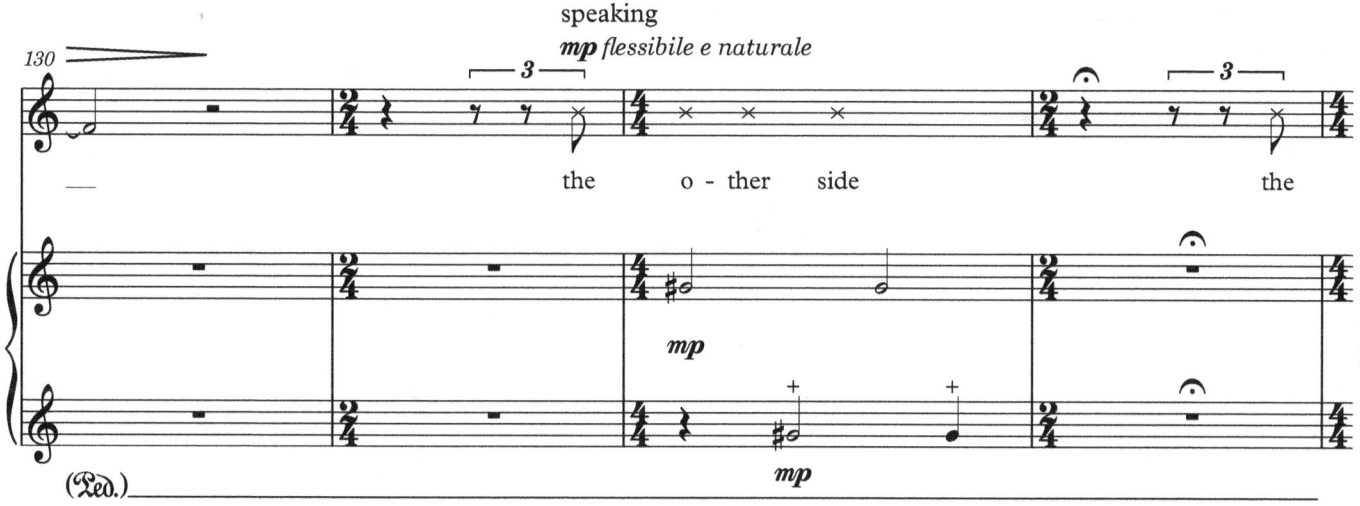

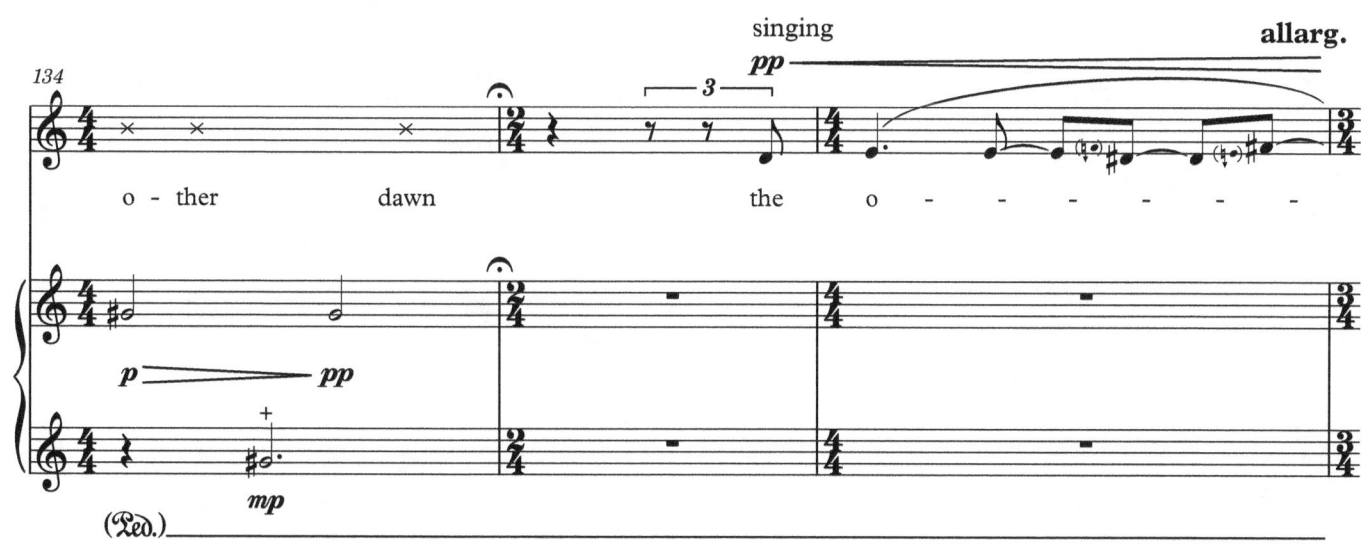

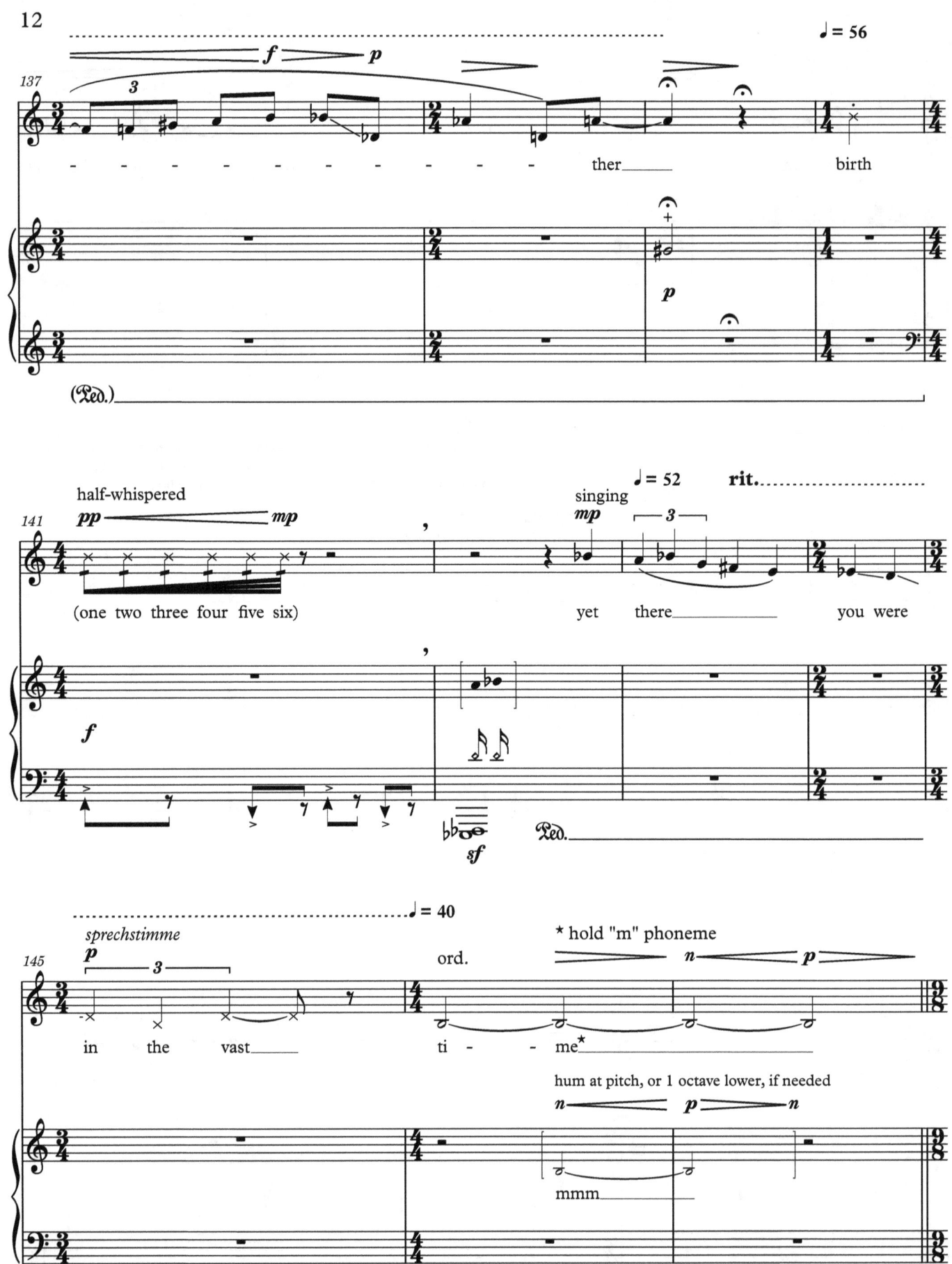

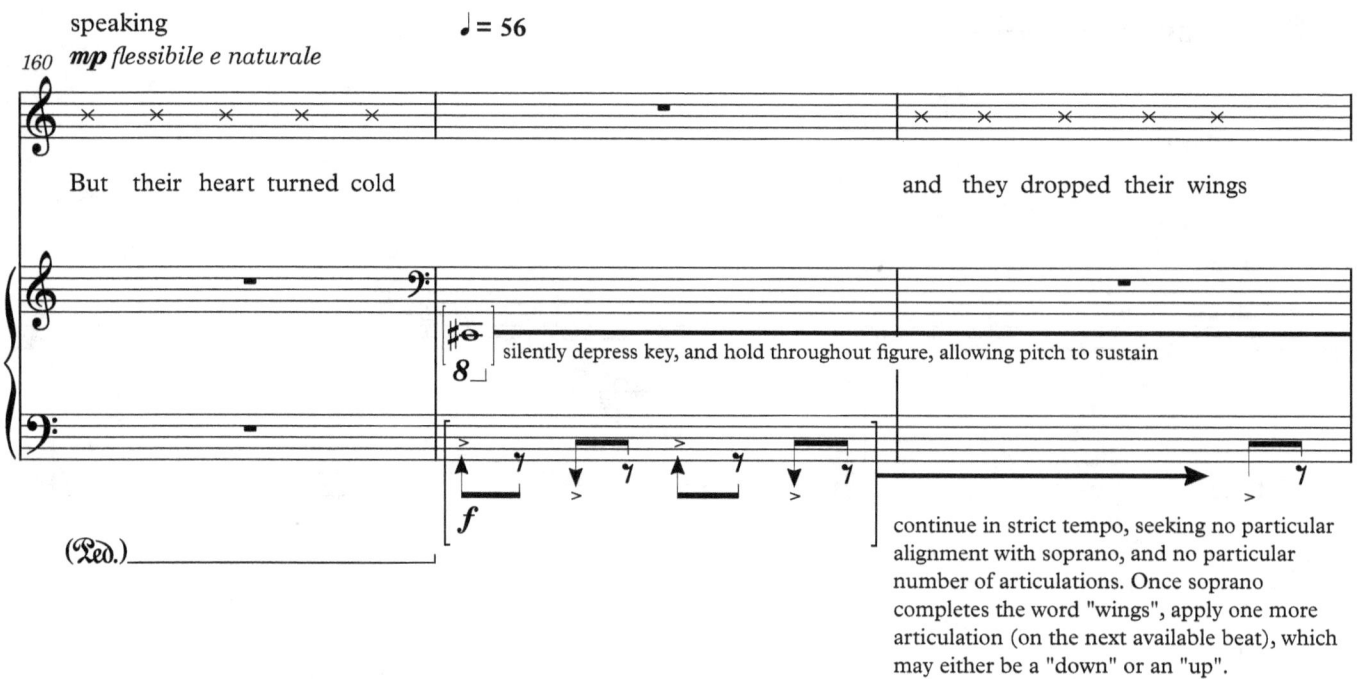
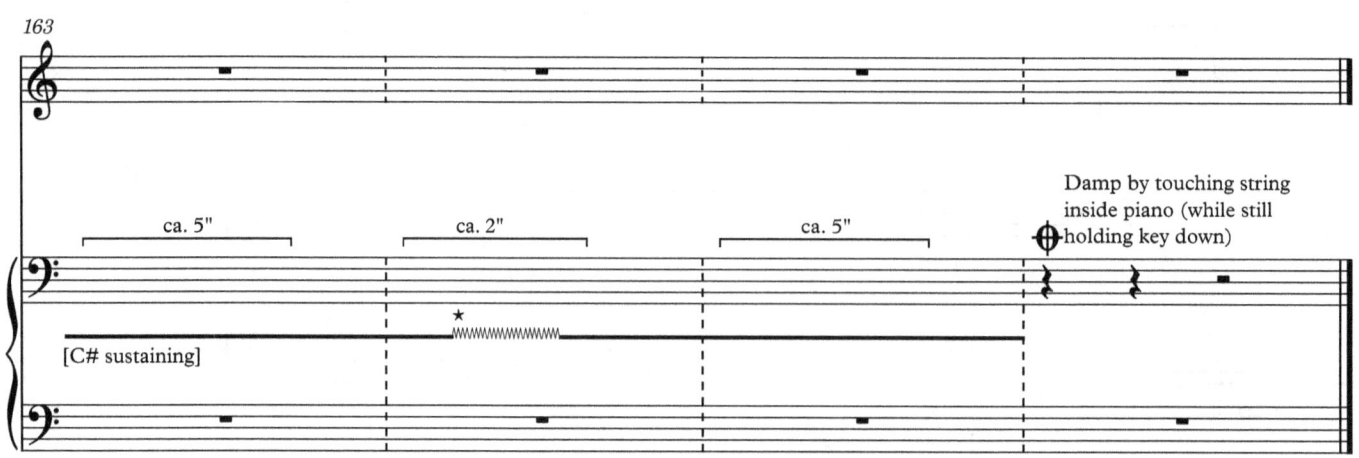

# The Best-Beloved

FRANCIS QUARLES

PAUL AYRES
(2005)

Copyright © 2005 by Paul Ayres. All Rights Reserved.

# Oh You Whom I Often and Silently Come

WALT WHITMAN

CLINT BORZONI
(2010)

Copyright © 2010 by Clint Borzoni. All Rights Reserved.

**a tempo   poco accel.**...............**Più mosso** (♩ = 67)

as I walk by your side   or sit near ____ or re-

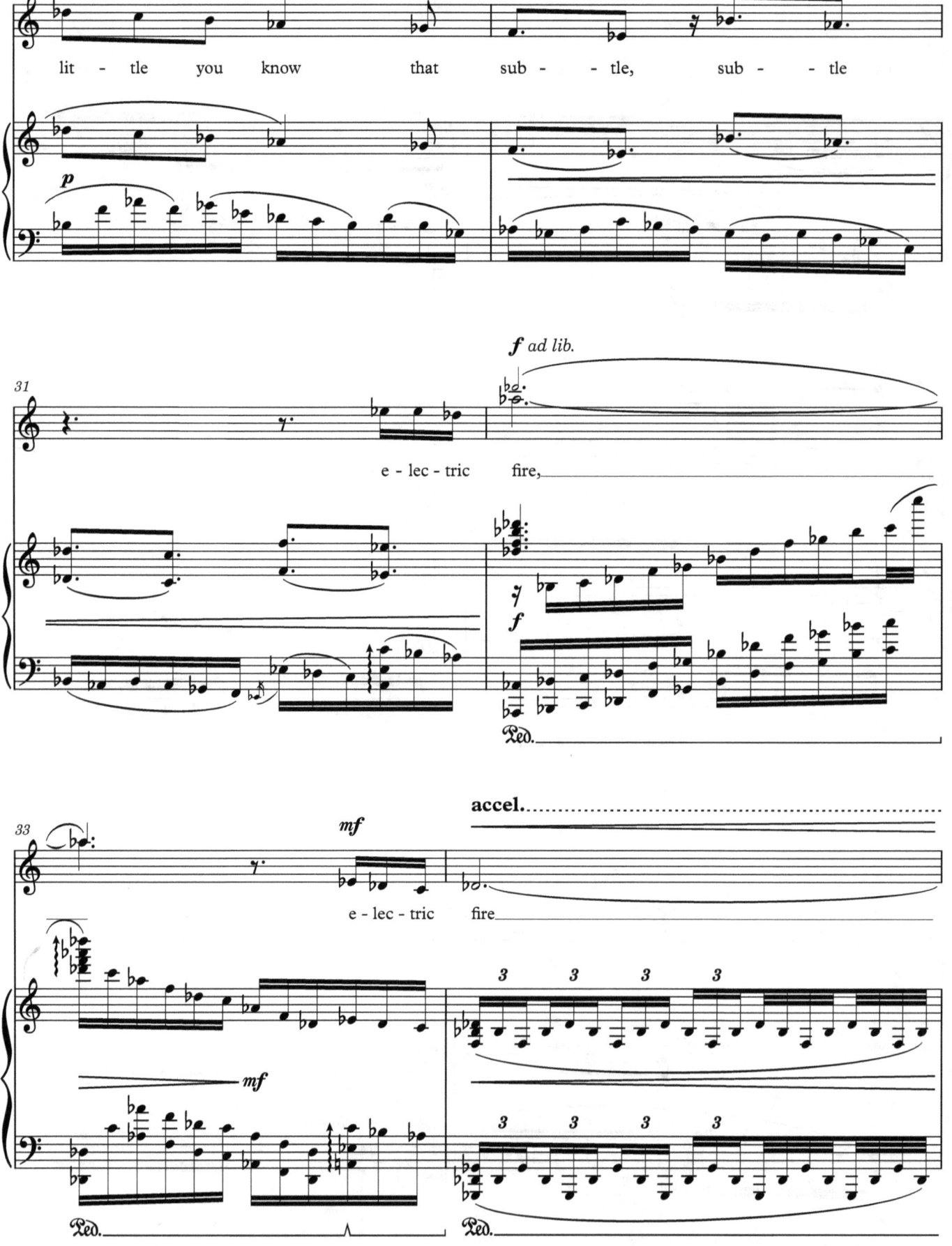

# Mr. Peck
## from The Tombstone Songs

TOMBSTONE EPITAPH

MARK BULLER
(2015)

Copyright © 2015 by Mark Buller (ASCAP). All Rights Reserved.

34

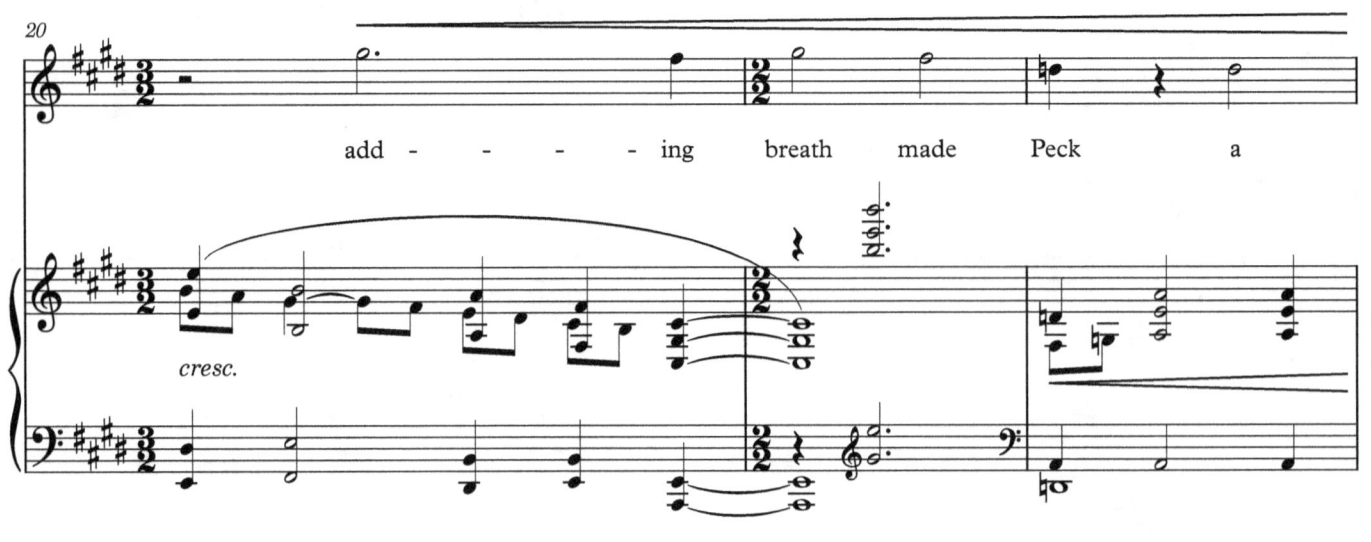
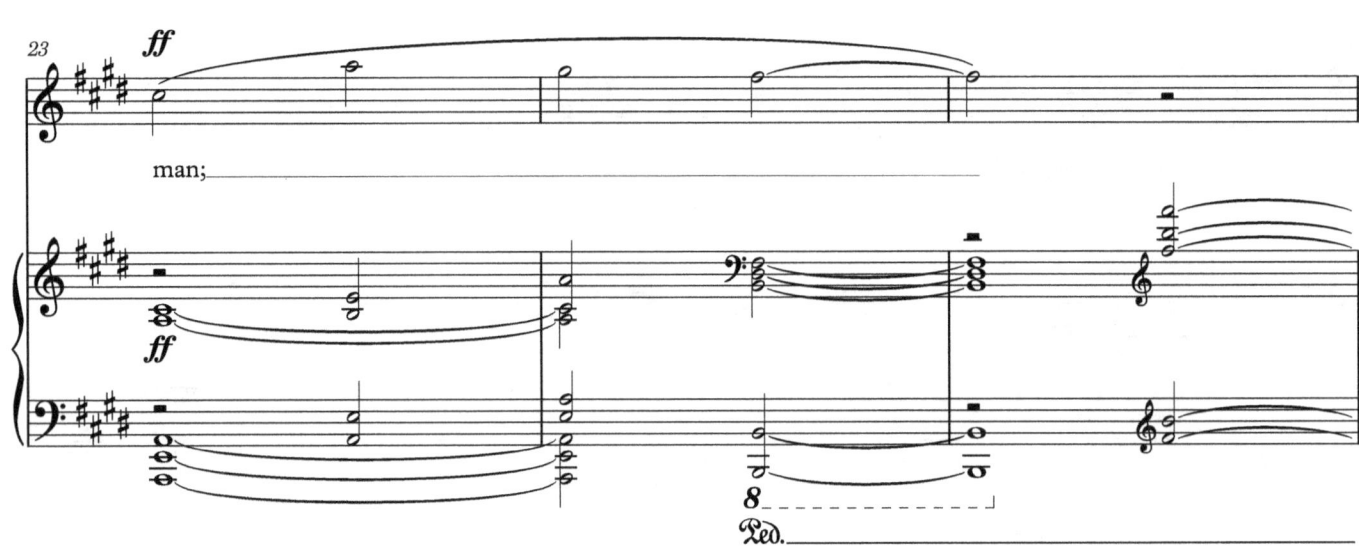

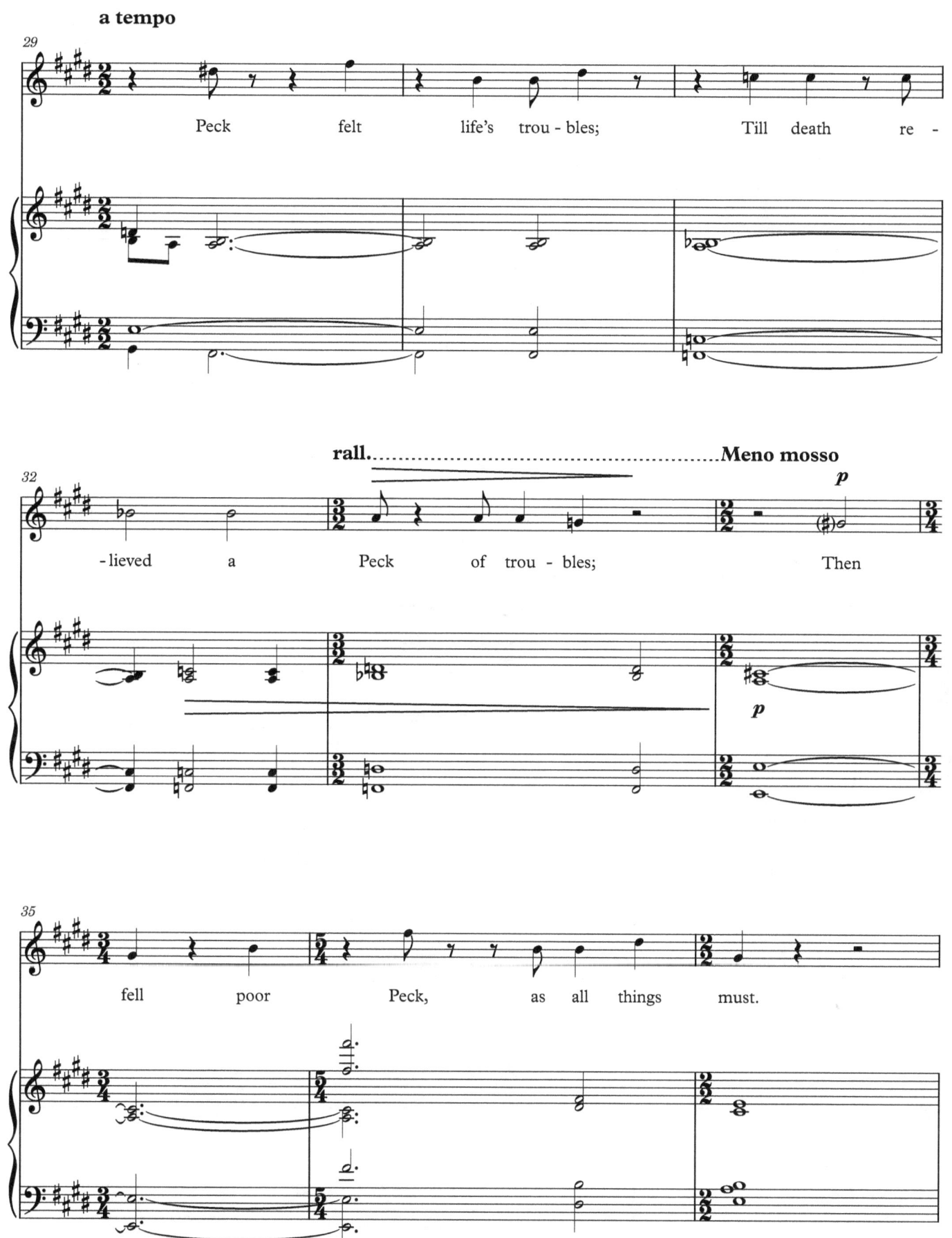

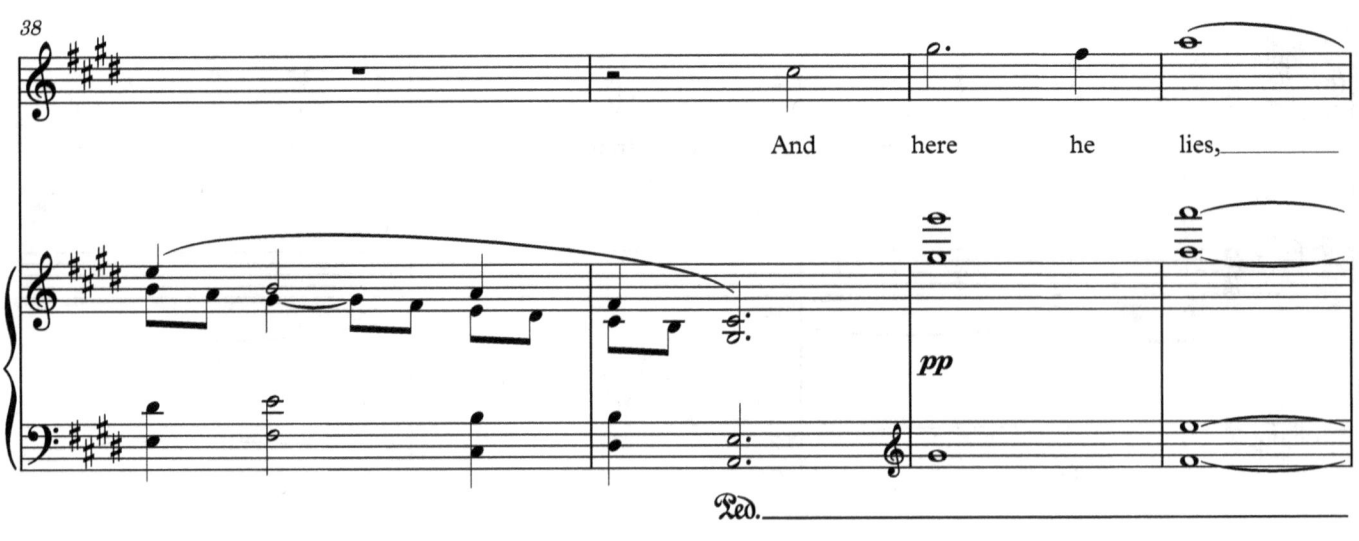
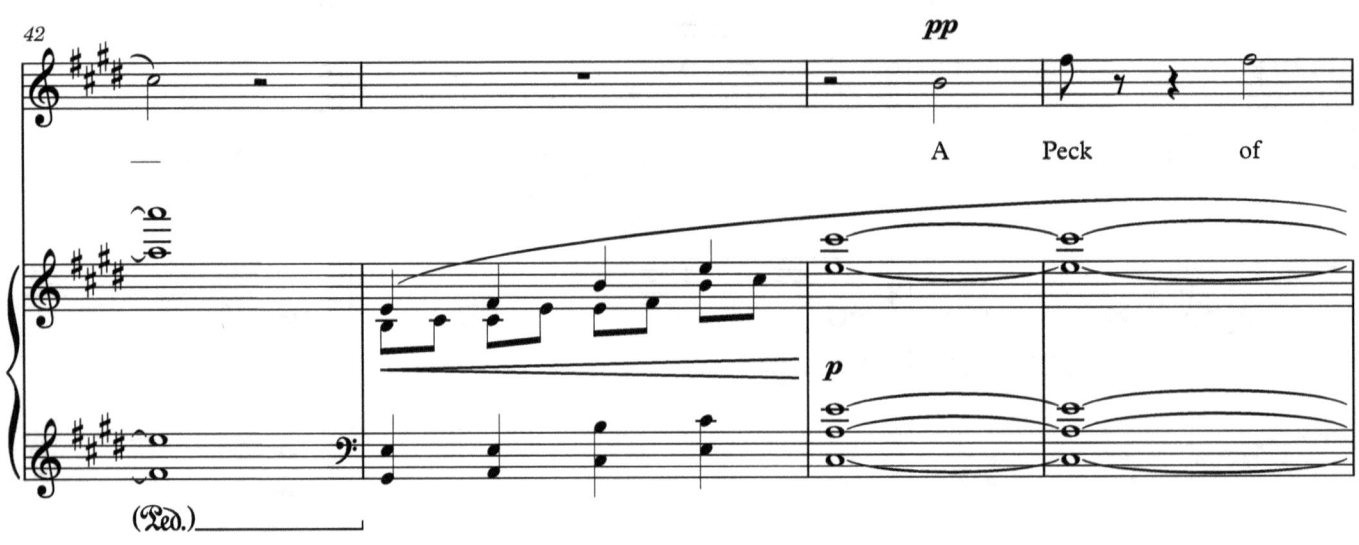

# Lovely Playthings
*from Three Gurney Songs*

IVOR GURNEY

MARTIN BUSSEY
(2005)

Copyright © 2005 Martin Bussey.

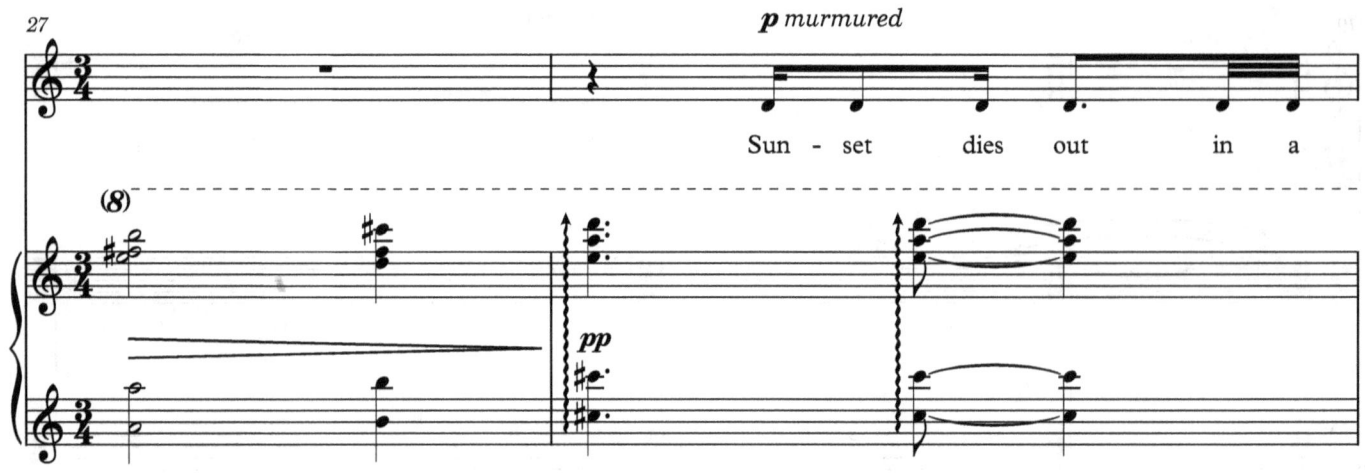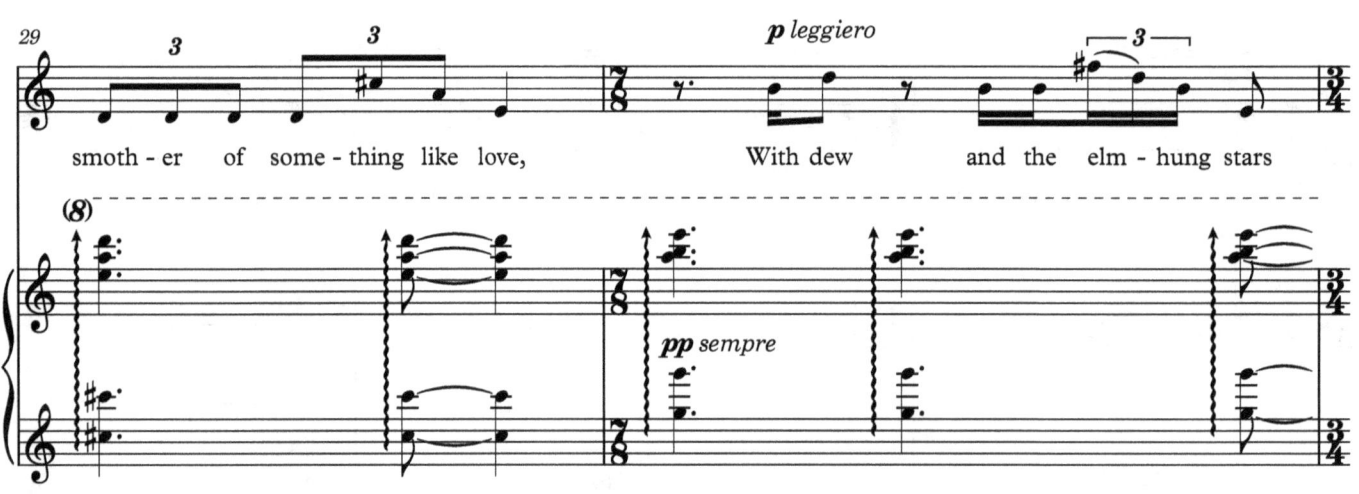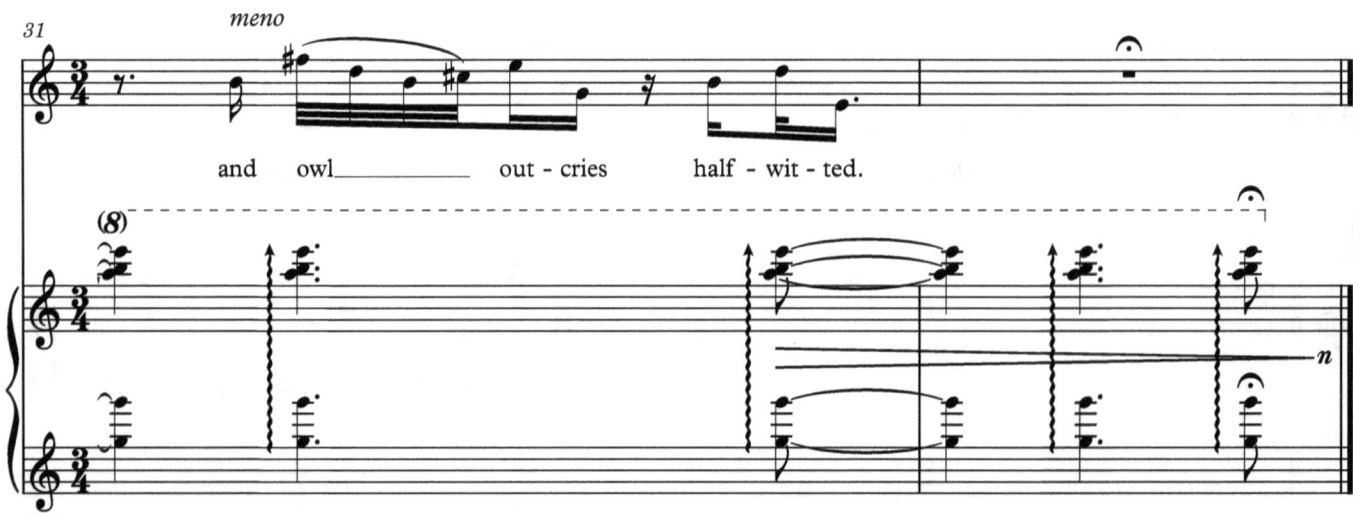

*Written and dedicated to Tess Altiveros, December 2013*
# He Wishes for the Cloths of Heaven

W.B. YEATS  EMERSON EADS
(2013)

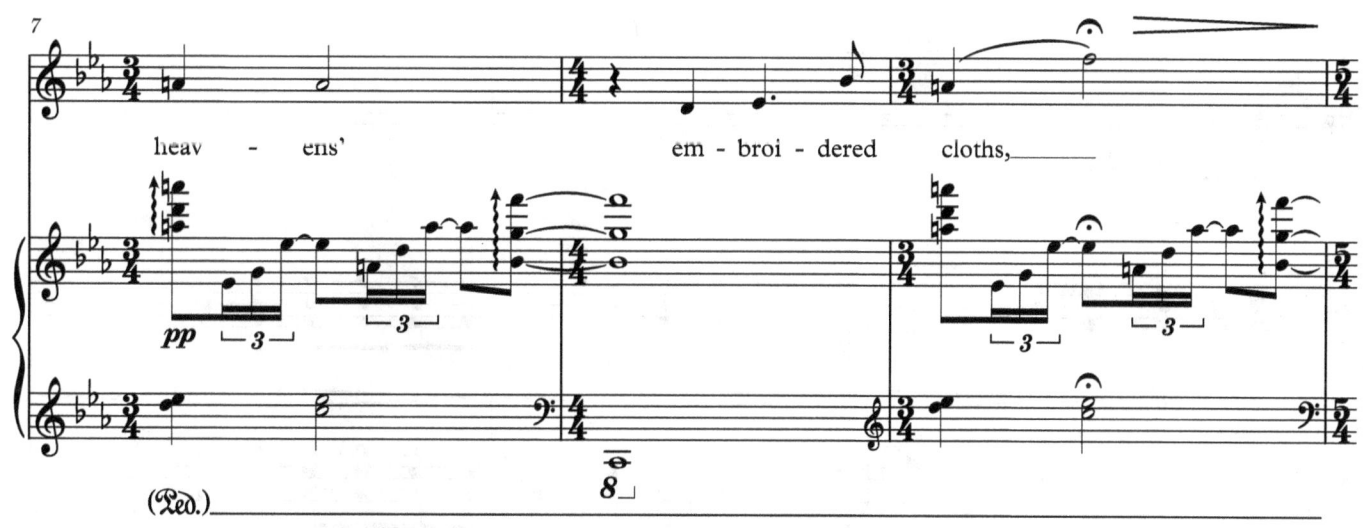

Copyright © 2013 by Emerson Eads. All Rights Reserved.

# Lullaby for a Baby Fairy

JOYCE KILMER

EVAN FEIN
(2011)

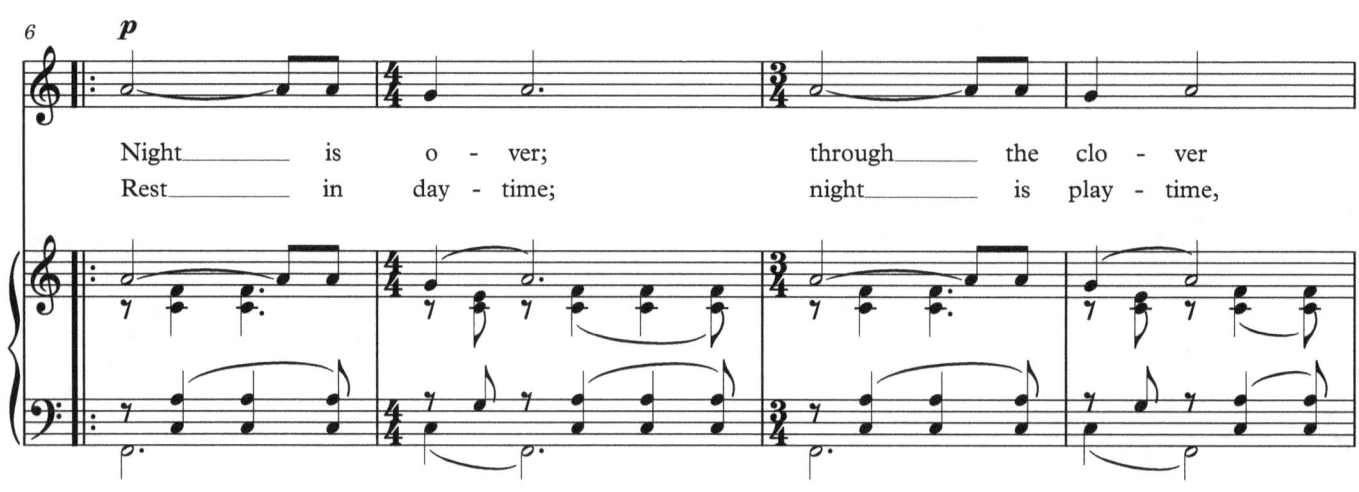

Copyright © MMXI Evan Fein (ASCAP). All rights reserved.

50

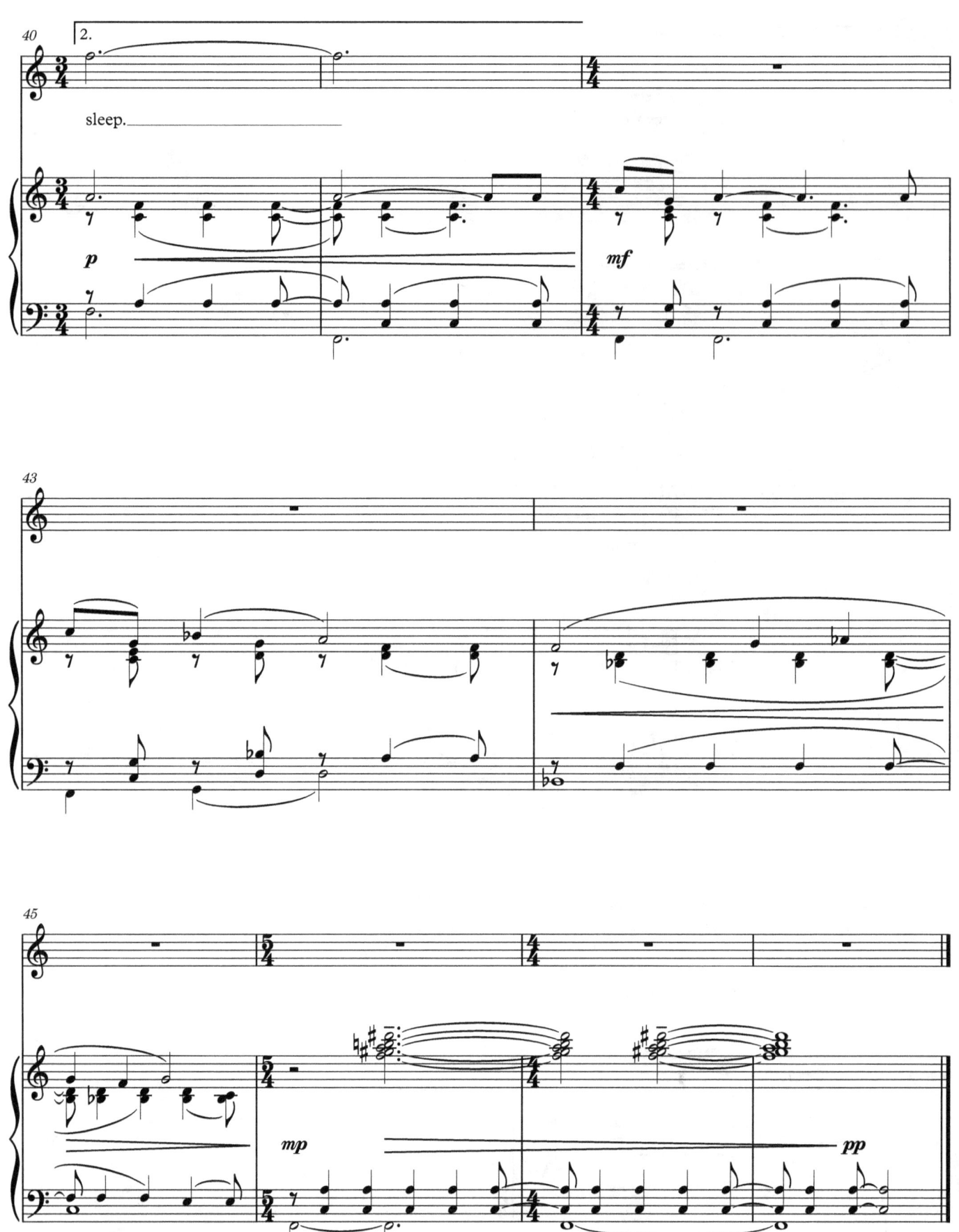

*for Amy Van Roekel*
# Dry Sandwiches

KATE GALE

DANIEL FELSENFELD
(2007)

Copyright © 2007 Felsenmusick Publishing Concern.
Text used with generous permission of Kate Gale.

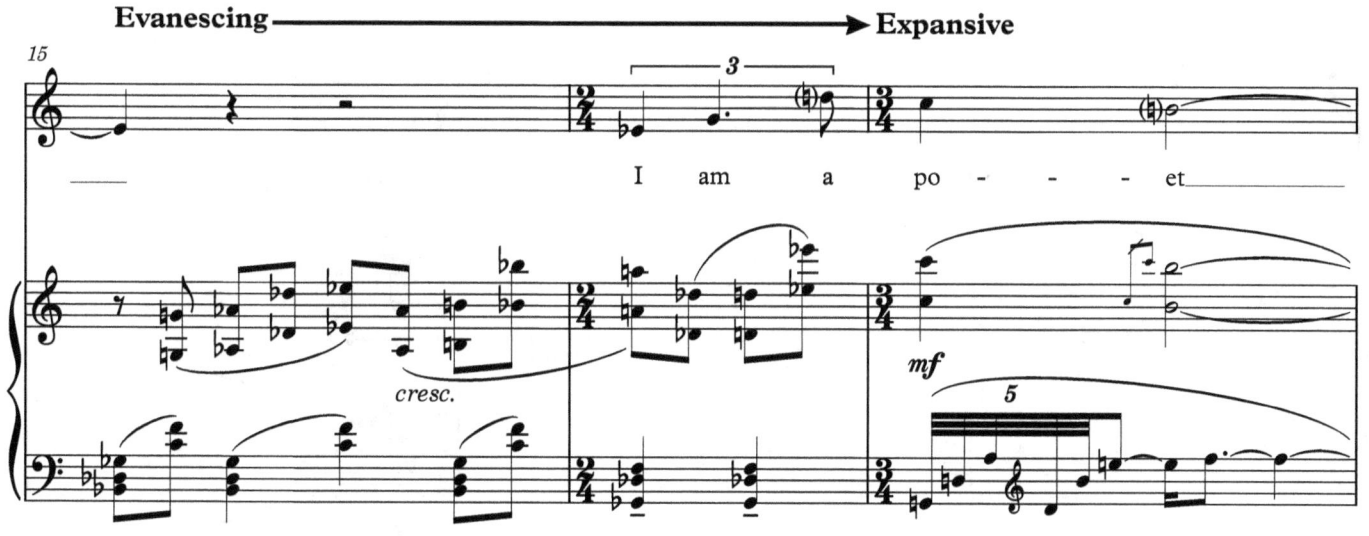

**Sharp**

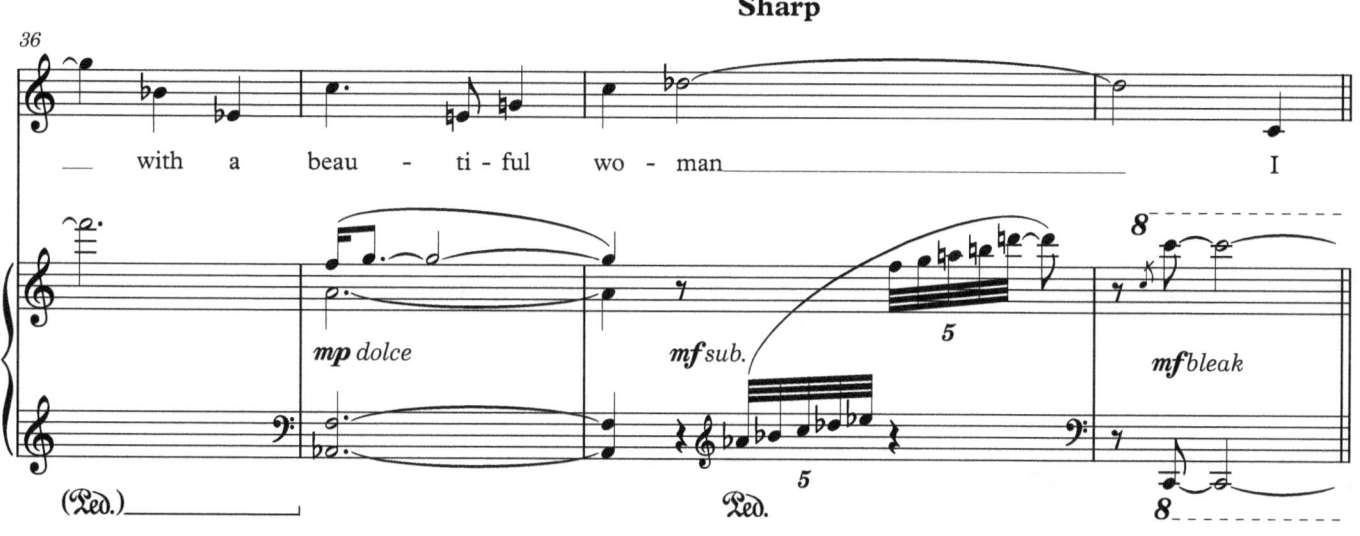

**Languid, creepy** (♩ = 52)

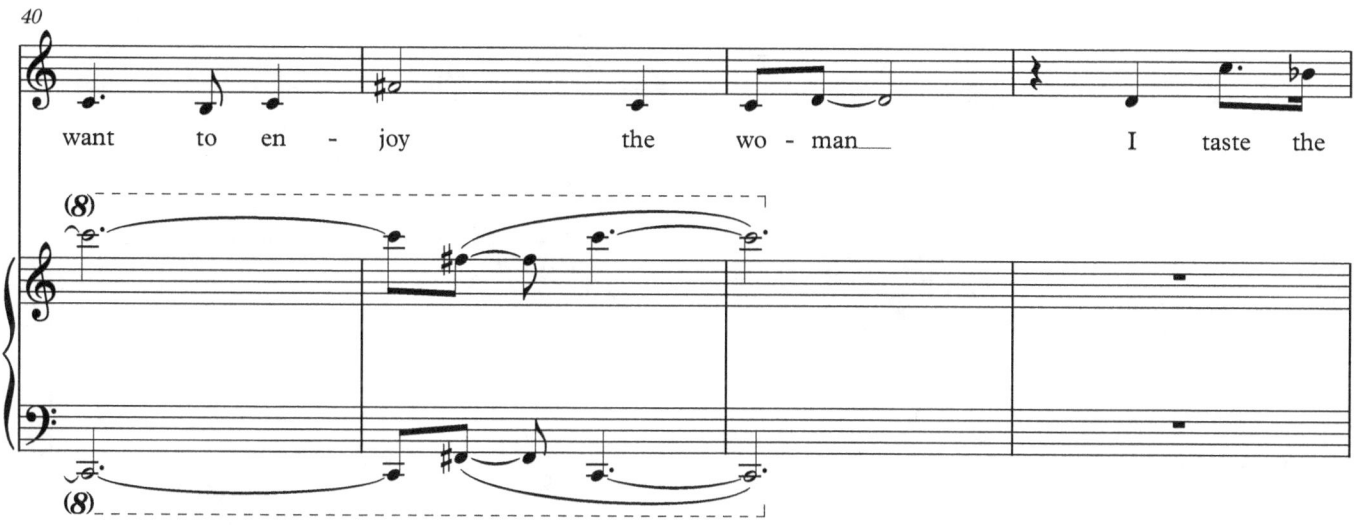

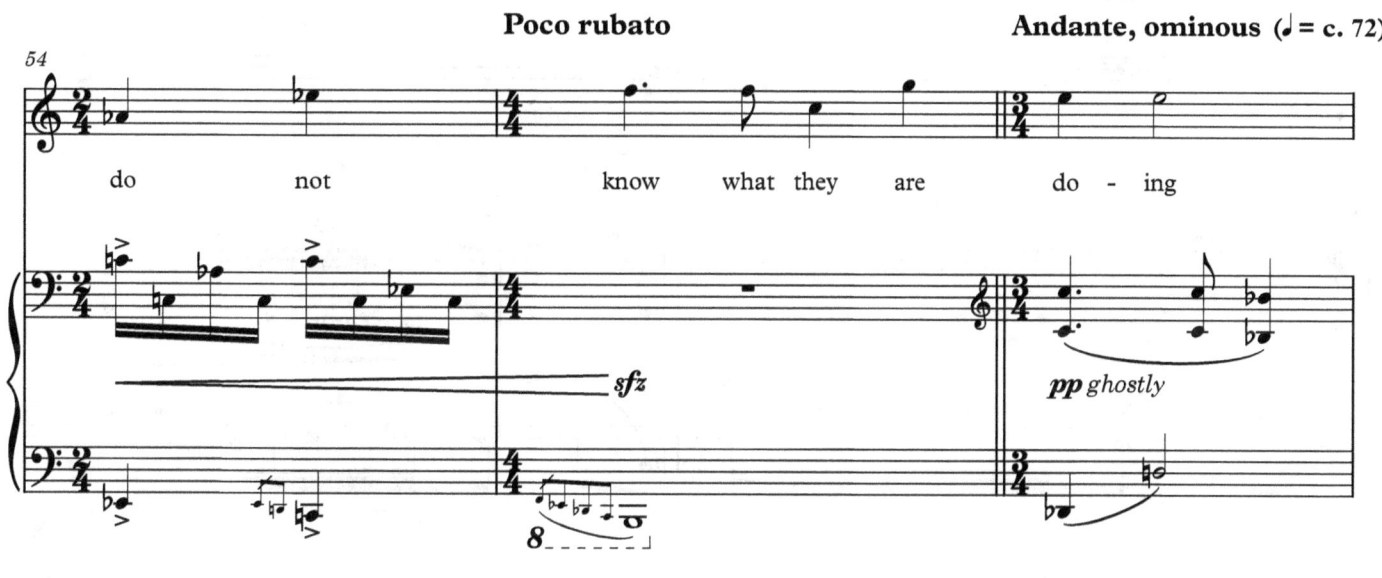

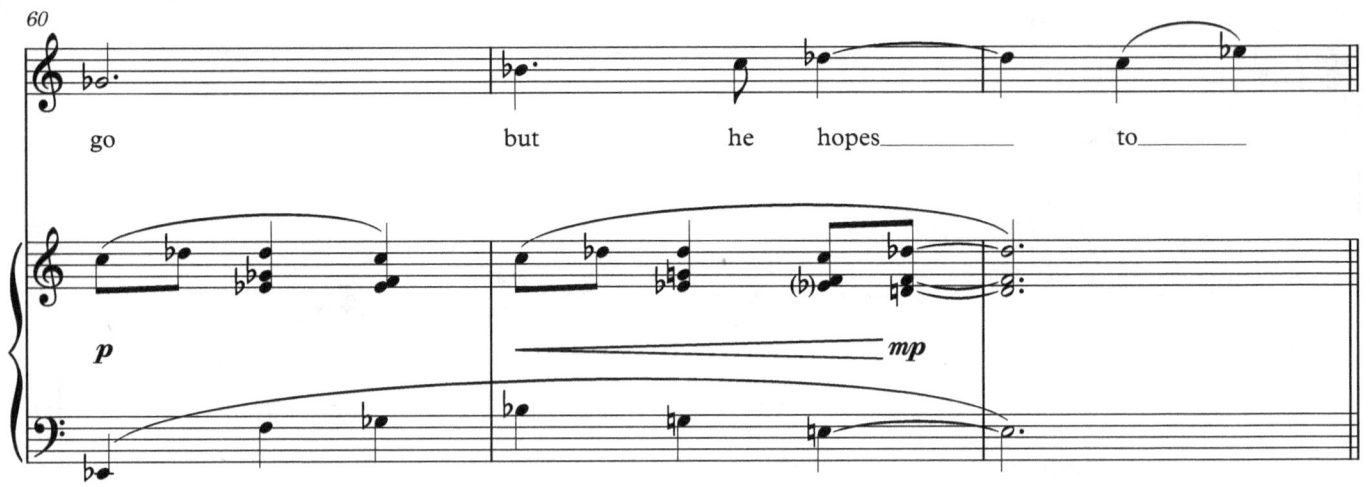

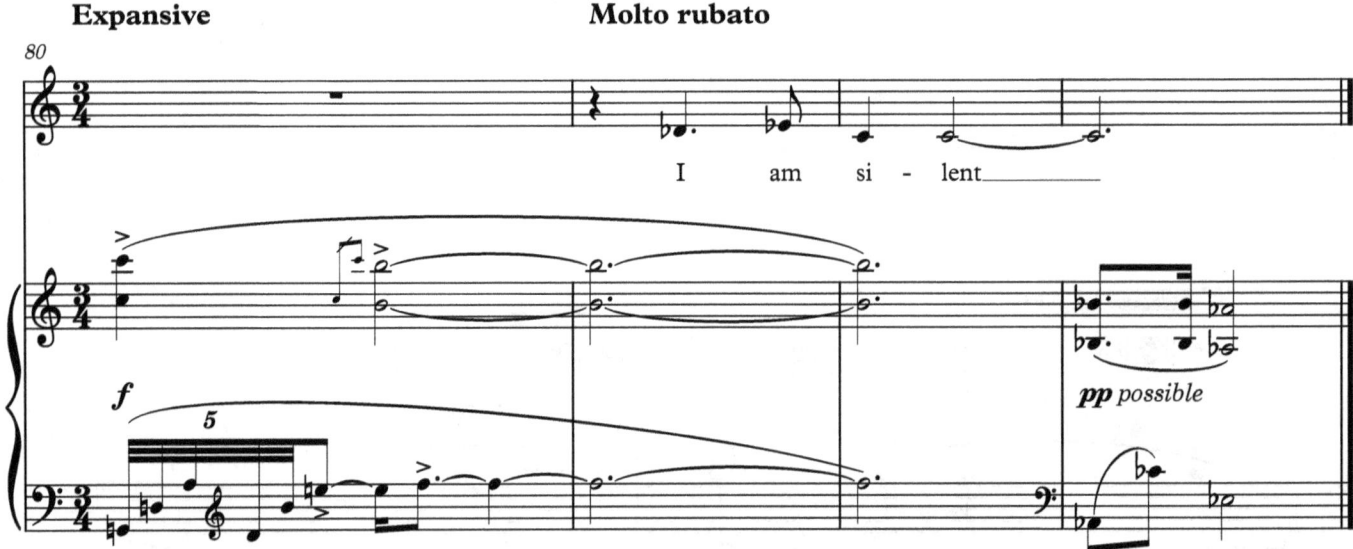

# The Storm

*from The Heart of the World*

SARA TEASDALE

JODI GOBLE
(2016)

Copyright © 2016 by Jodi Goble. All Rights Reserved.

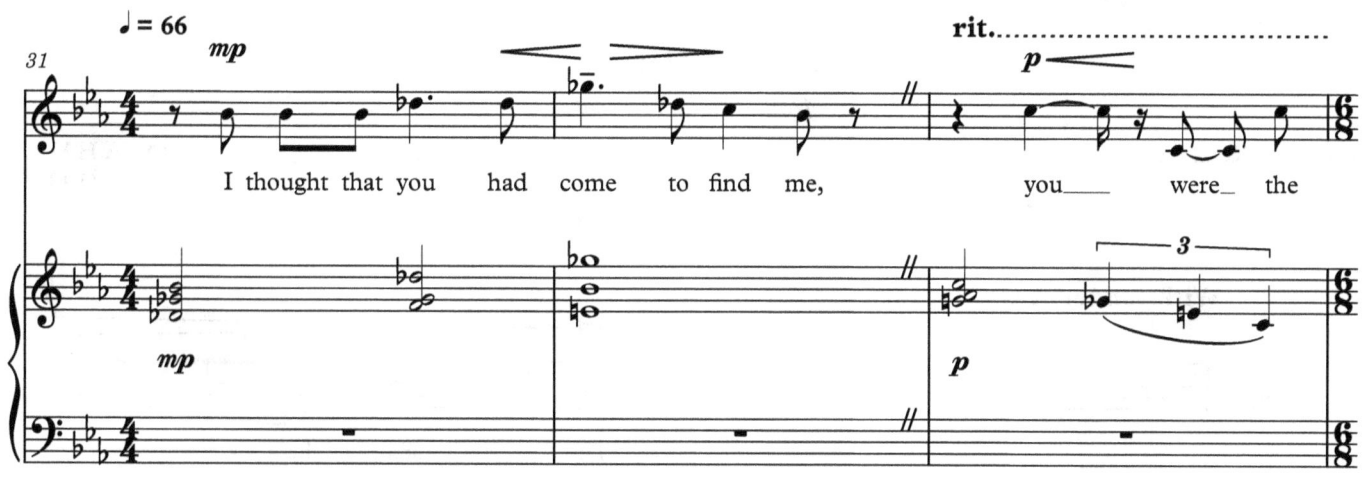

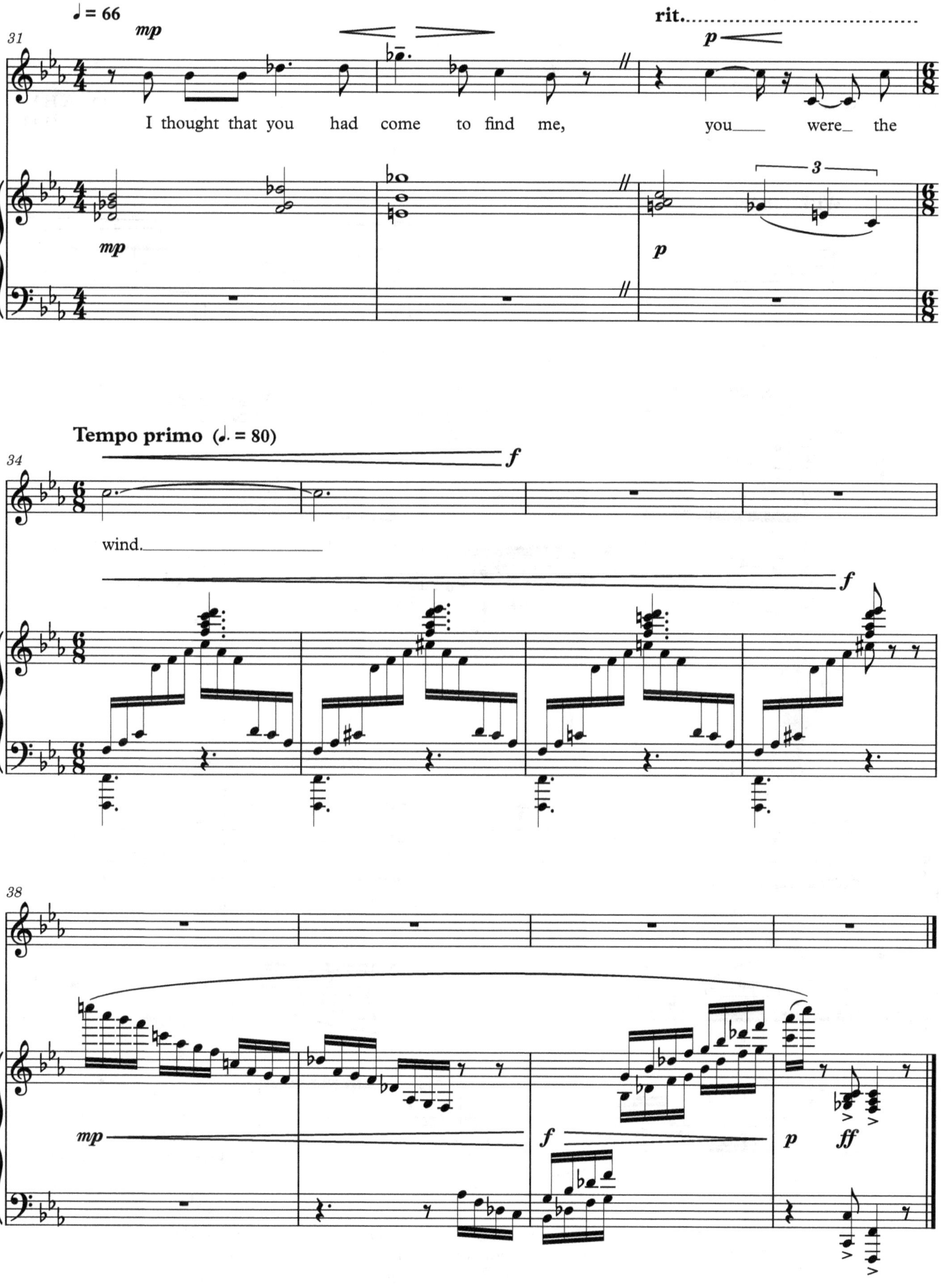
♩ = 66
rit.
Tempo primo (♩. = 80)
I thought that you had come to find me,
you were the
wind.

# Song

*from Night Dances*

EMILY BRONTË

JULIANA HALL
(1987)

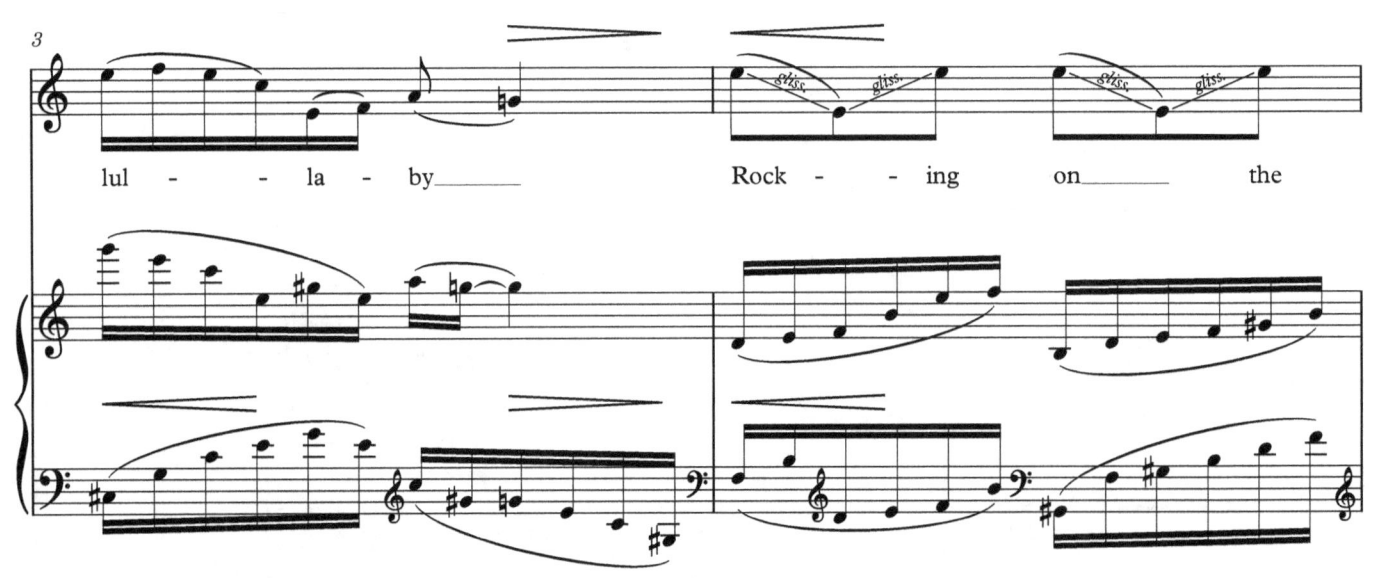

Music: Copyright © Juliana Hall Music. Copyright transferred 2017 to E.C. Schirmer Music Company, Inc.
Copyright © 2017 by E.C. Schirmer Music Company, Inc., a division of ECS Publishing Group. www.ecspublishing.com
All rights reserved. Reprinted by permission.

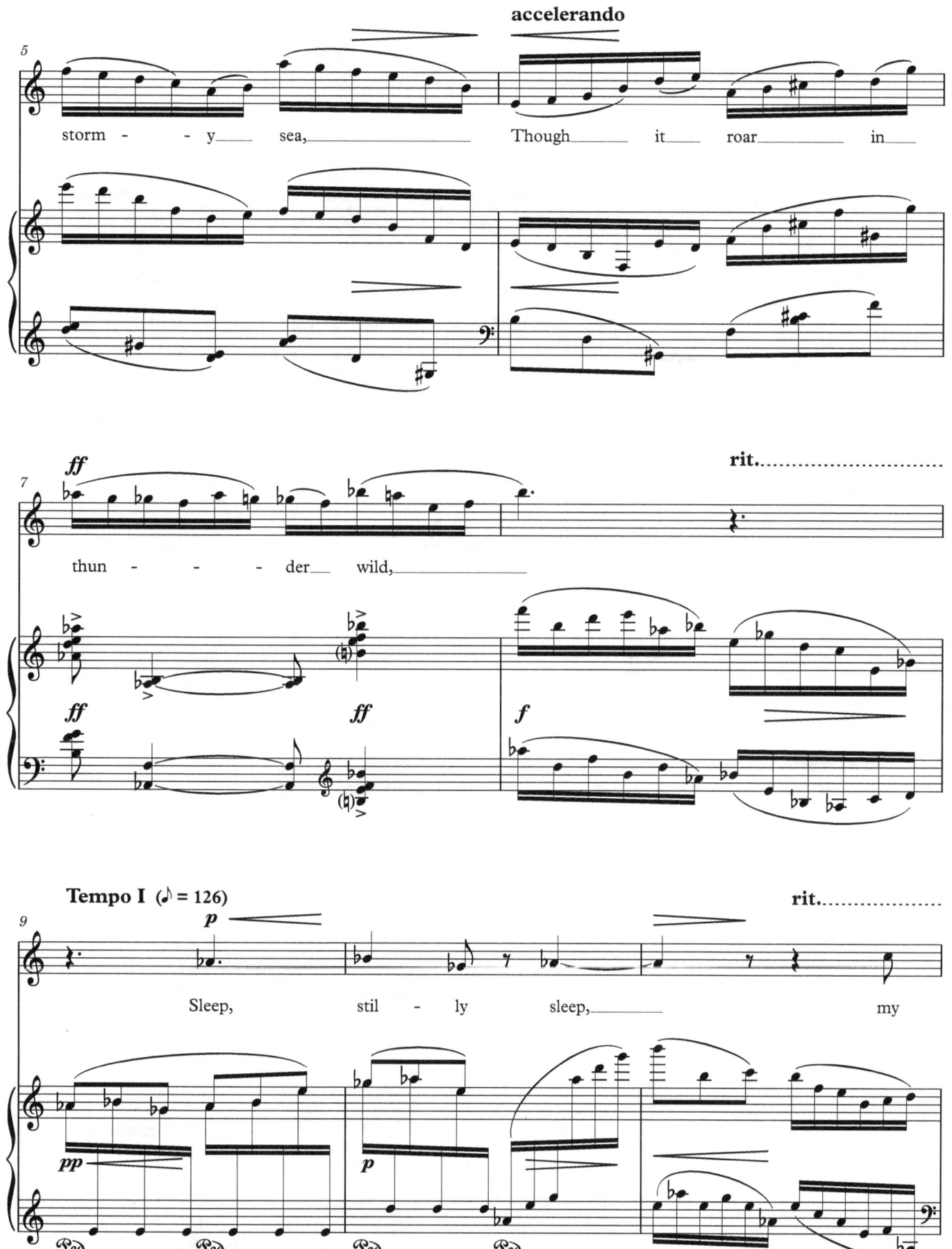

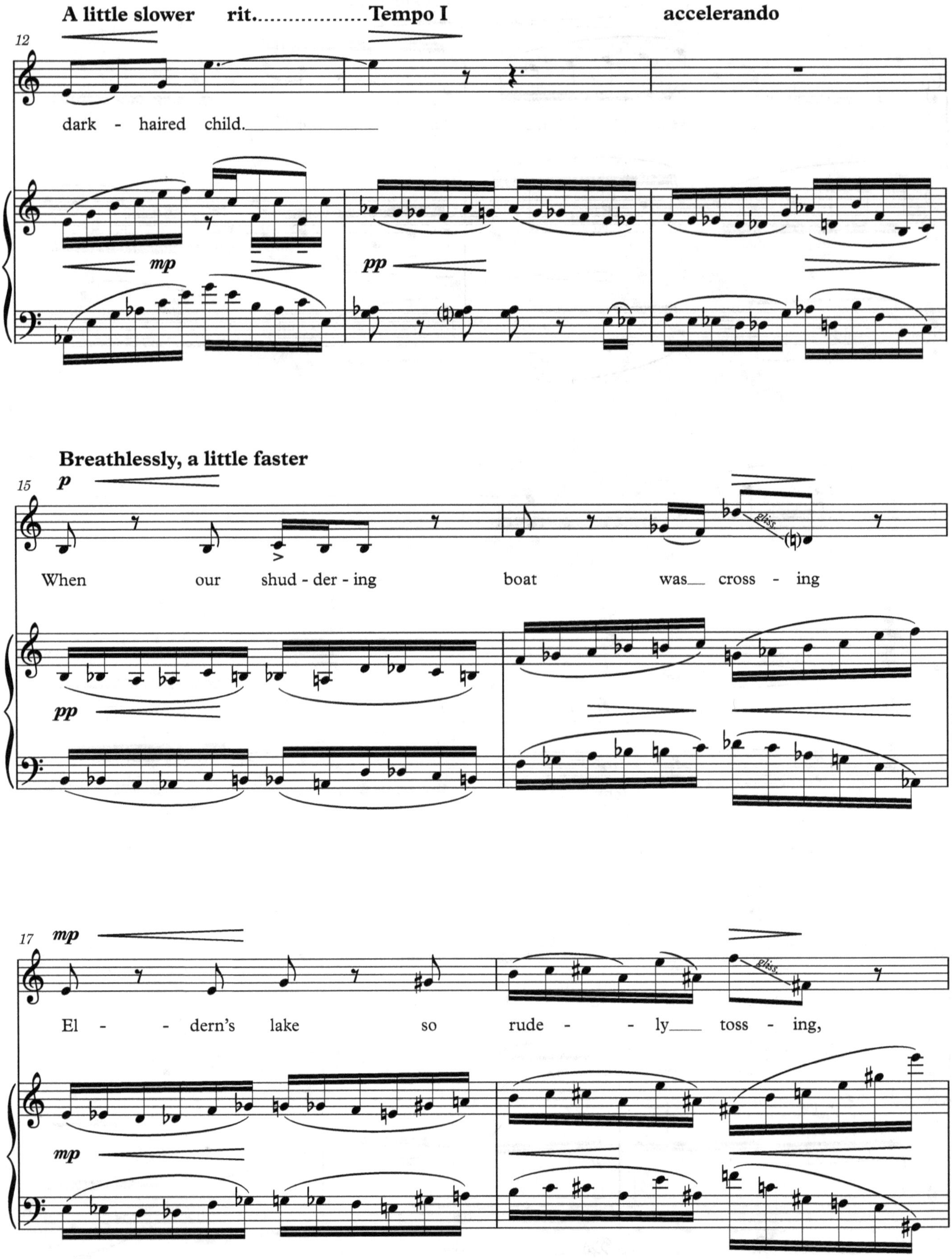

68

**A little slower**  rit.............**Tempo I**   accelerando

dark - haired child.

**Breathlessly, a little faster**

When our shud-der-ing boat was crossing

El - dern's lake so rude - ly toss - ing,

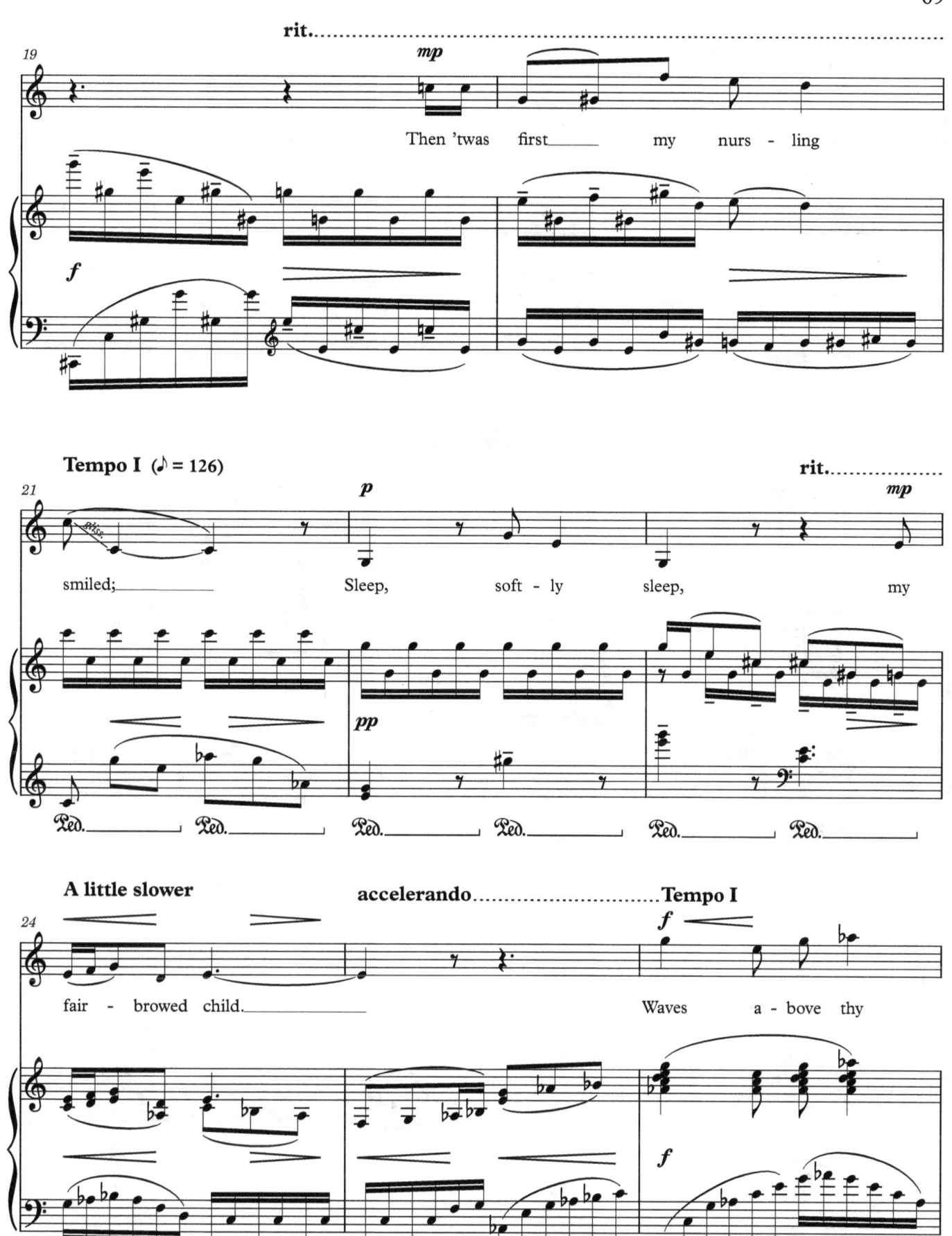

# Canto of the Leaves (Empyrean)

JOHN KINSELLA

GORDON KERRY
(2009)

Copyright © 2009 Gordon Kerry. All Rights Reserved.

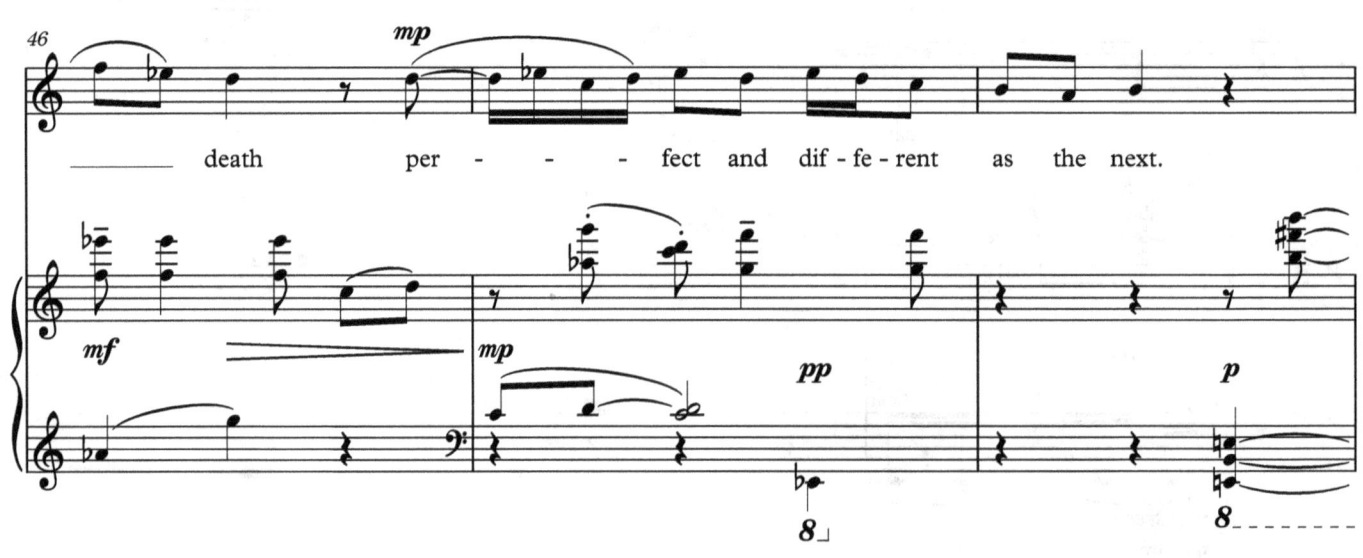

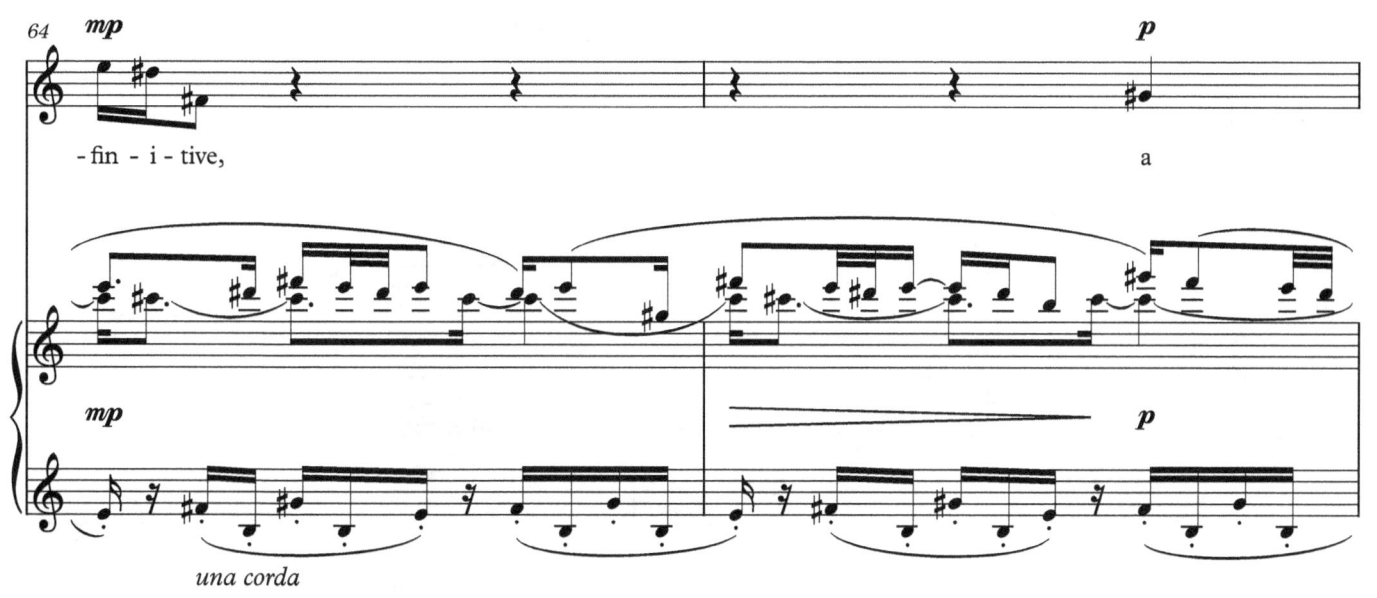

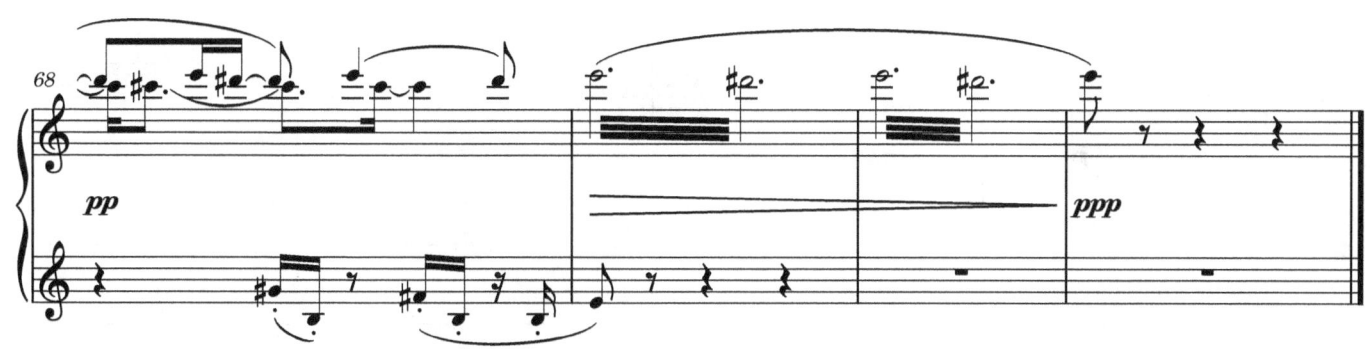

# Fall, Leaves, Fall

EMILY BRONTË  JOSHUA ALAN LINDSAY
(2017)

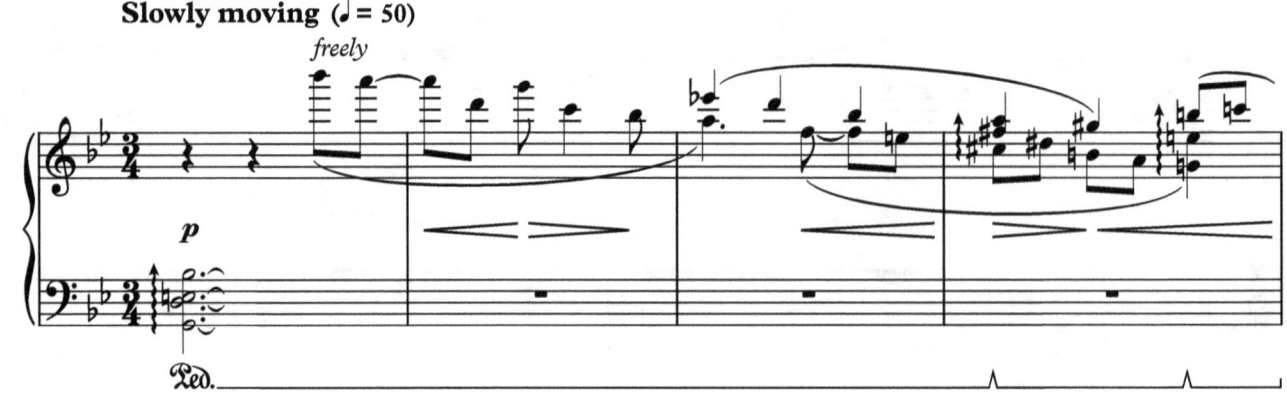

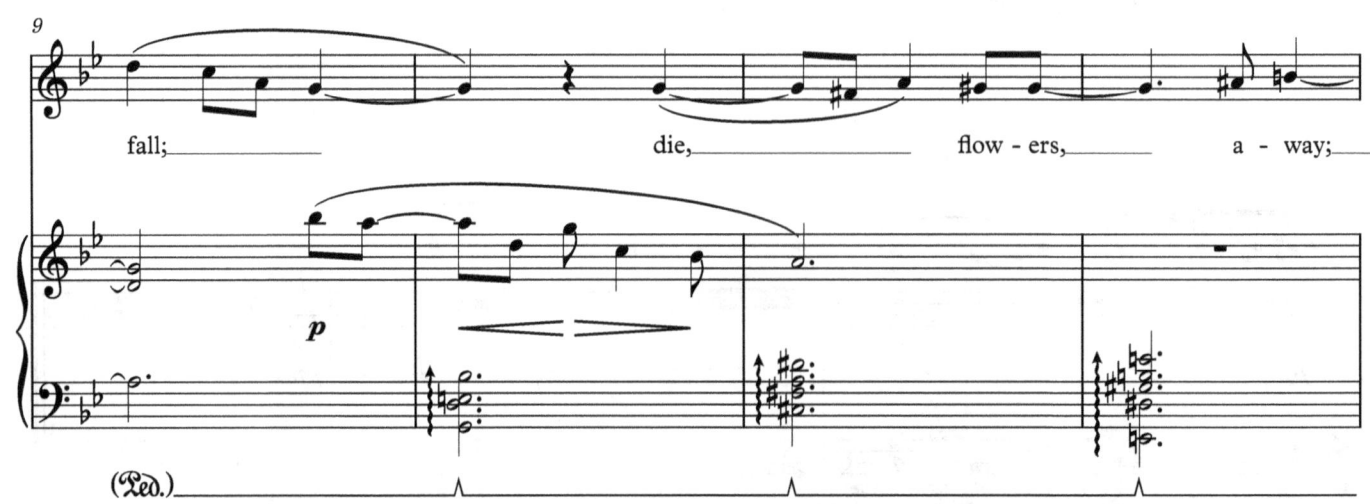

Music copyright © 2017 by Joshua Alan Lindsay. All Rights Reserved.

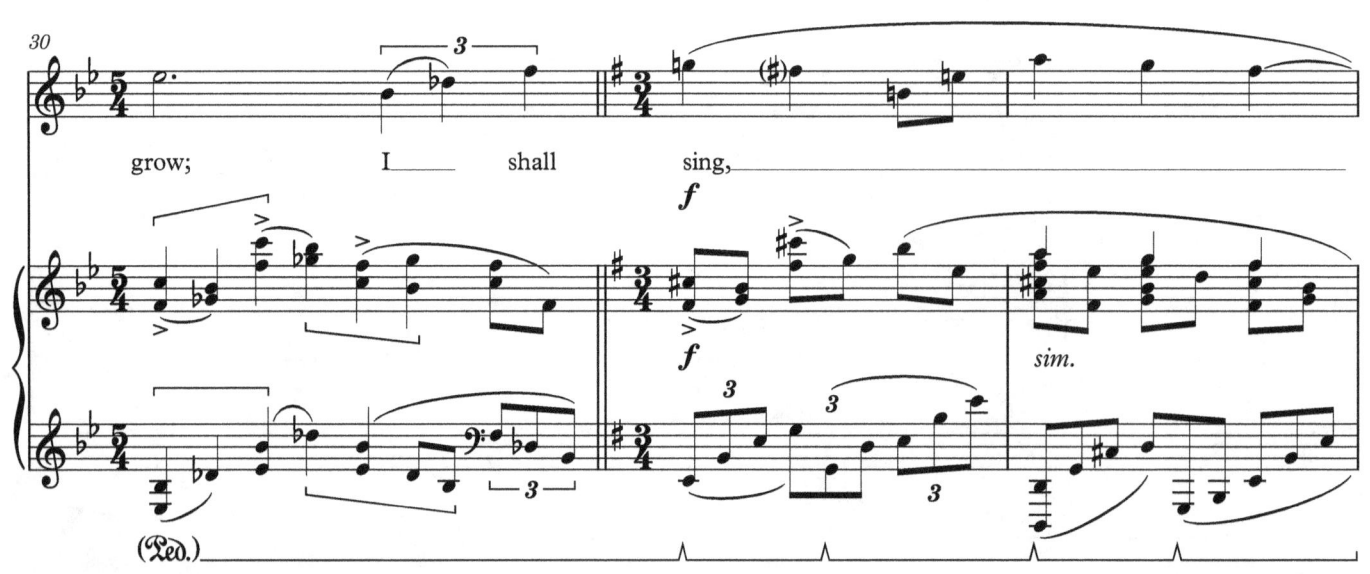

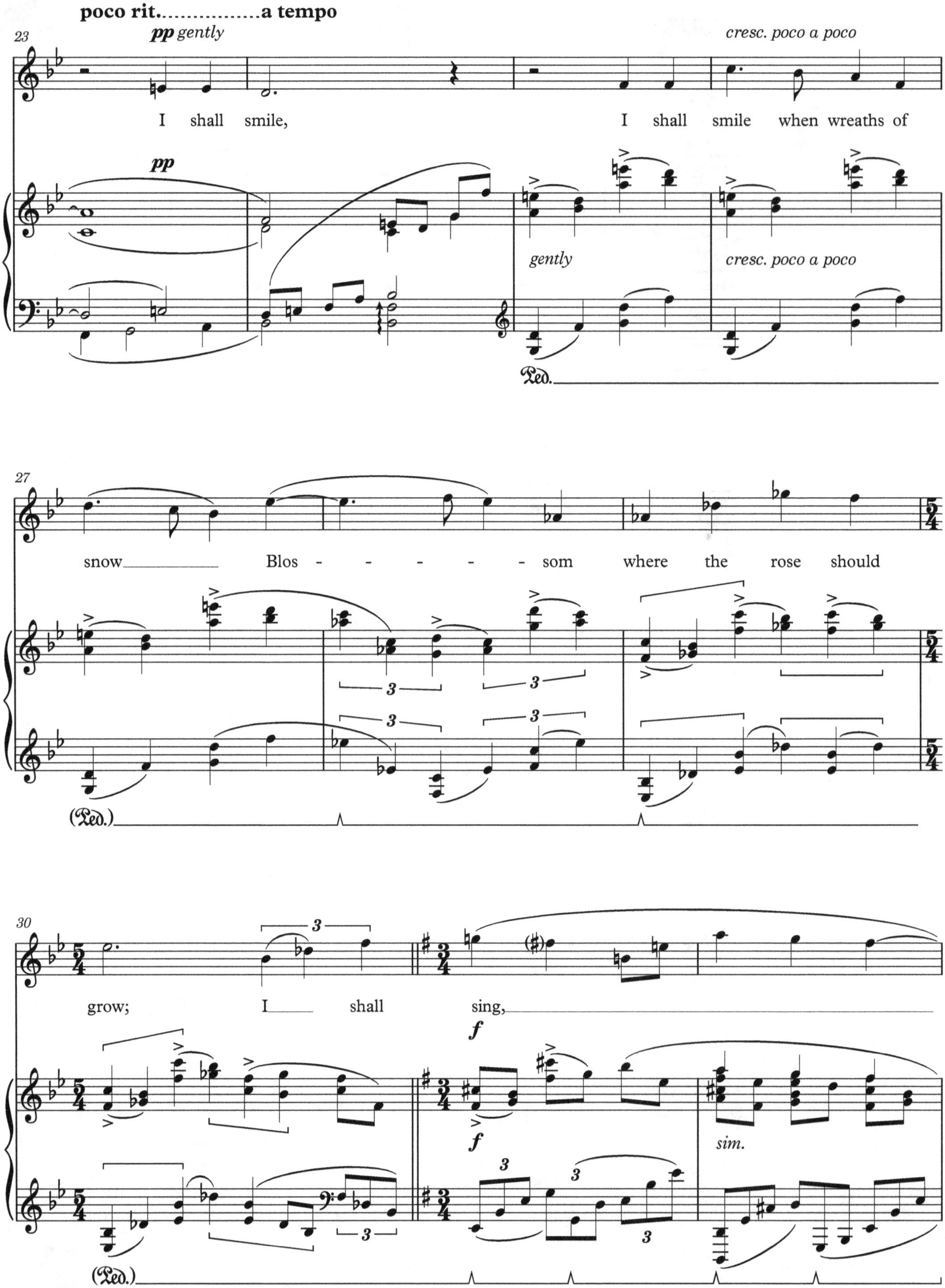
poco rit................a tempo
pp gently
cresc. poco a poco
I shall smile, I shall smile when wreaths of
pp
gently
cresc. poco a poco
Ped.
snow Blos - - - - - - som where the rose should
(Ped.)
grow; I shall sing,
f
f
sim.
(Ped.)

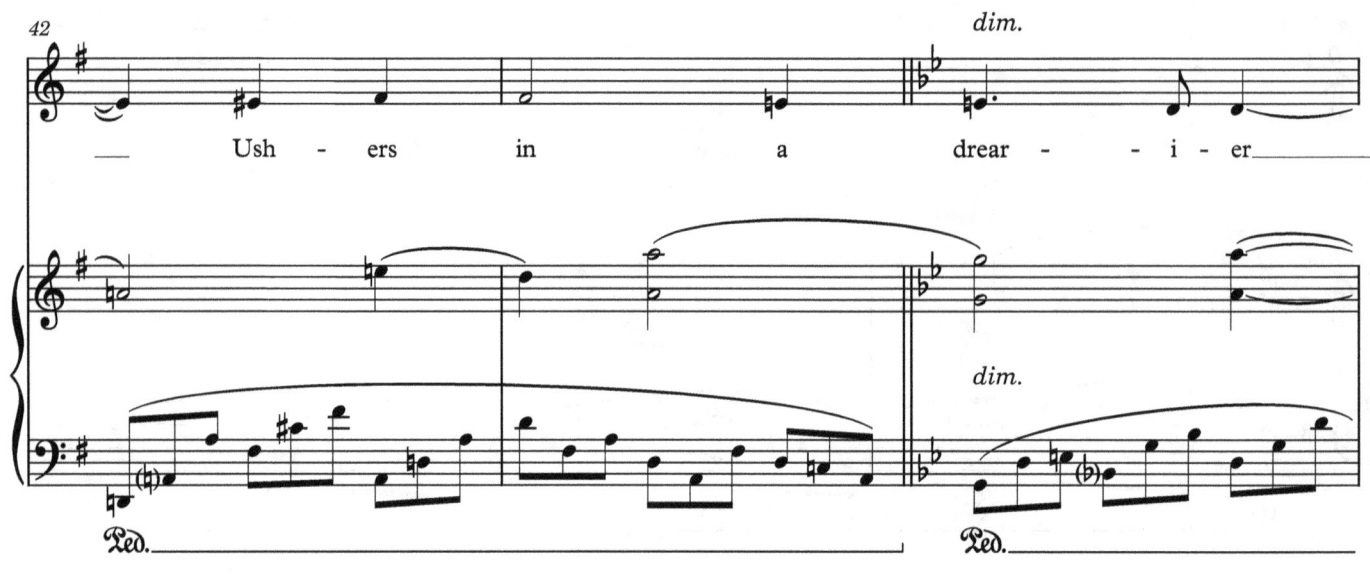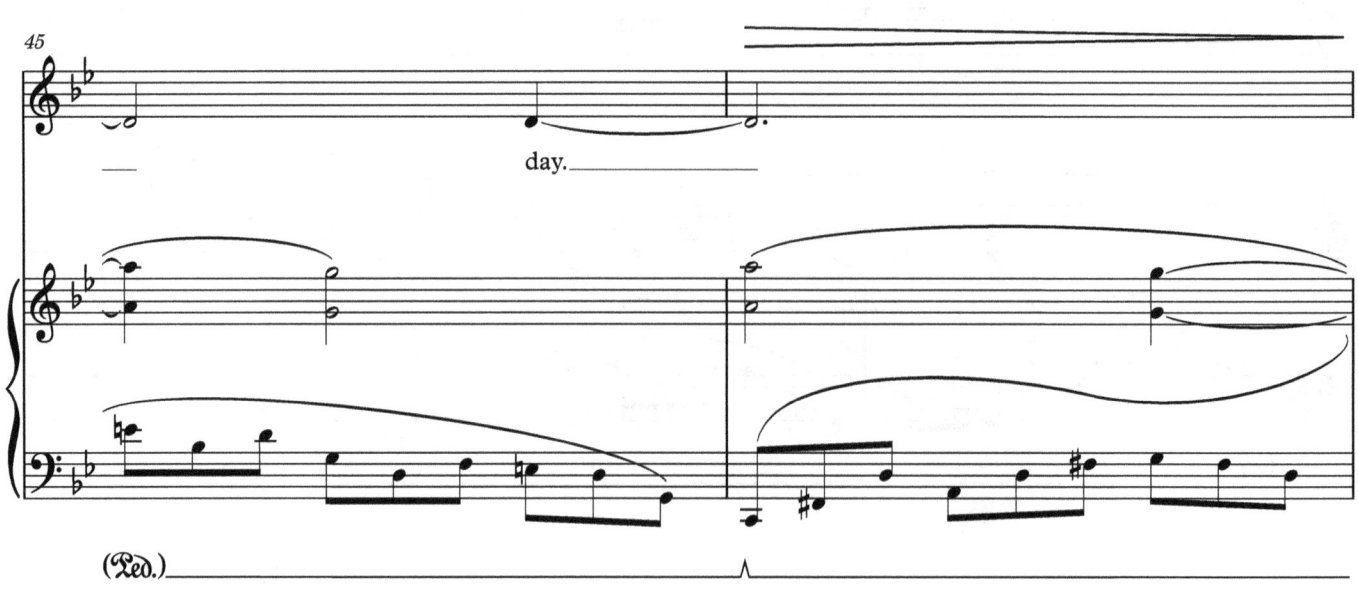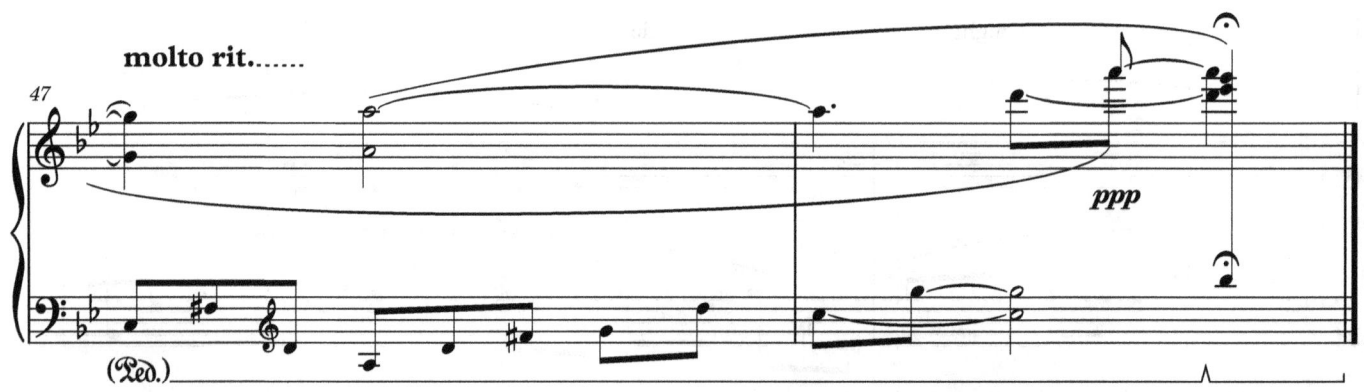

*for Alexandra Smither*

# Penelope

Music and text by
CECILIA LIVINGSTON
(2014)

*let the decay dictate the length of the silences*
*for an echoing, murmuring effect*

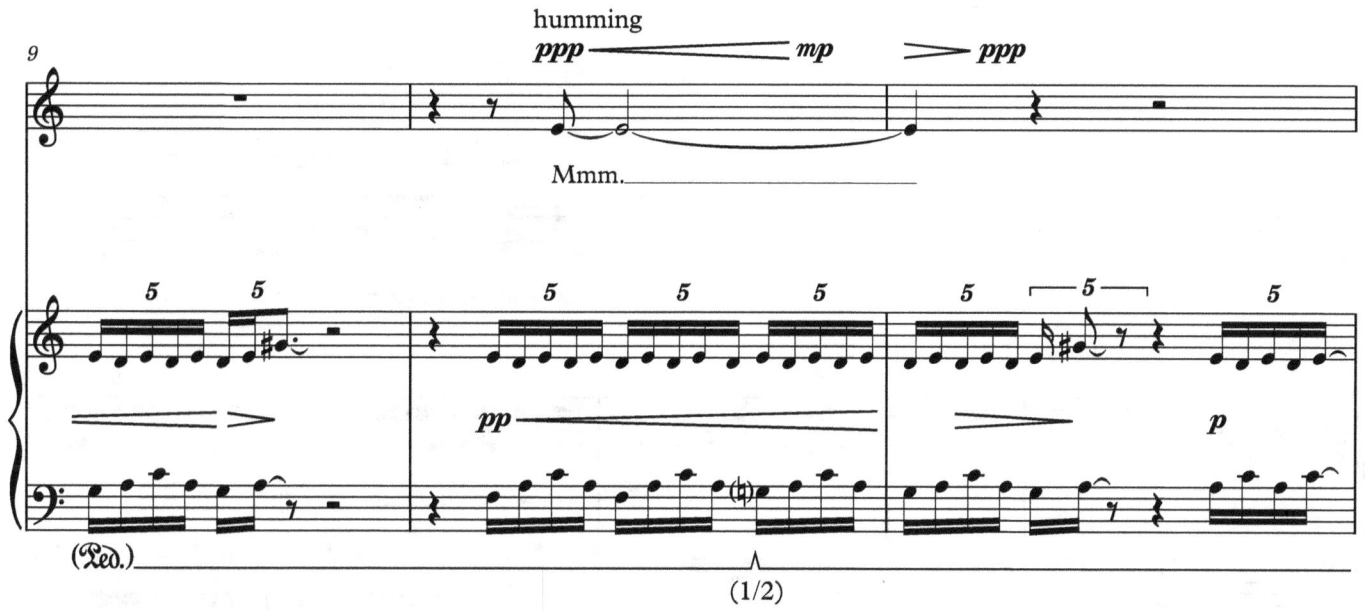

(1/2)

Copyright © 2014 by Cecilia Livingston. All Rights Reserved.

What_ is it,___ to be wait - ing?___ What_ is it___
___ to be wait - ing___ for you? Is it want - ing?
Is it lov - ing? Is it mov - ing through me like a fire?
accel.
pp p mf
(Ped.)
(1/2)

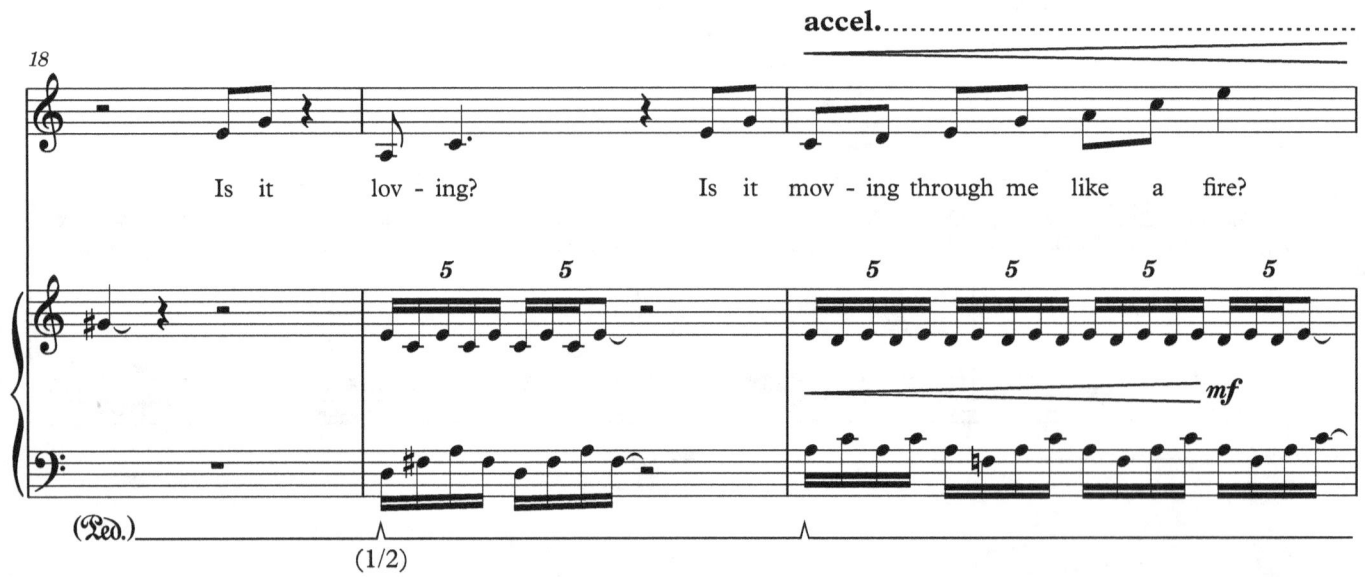

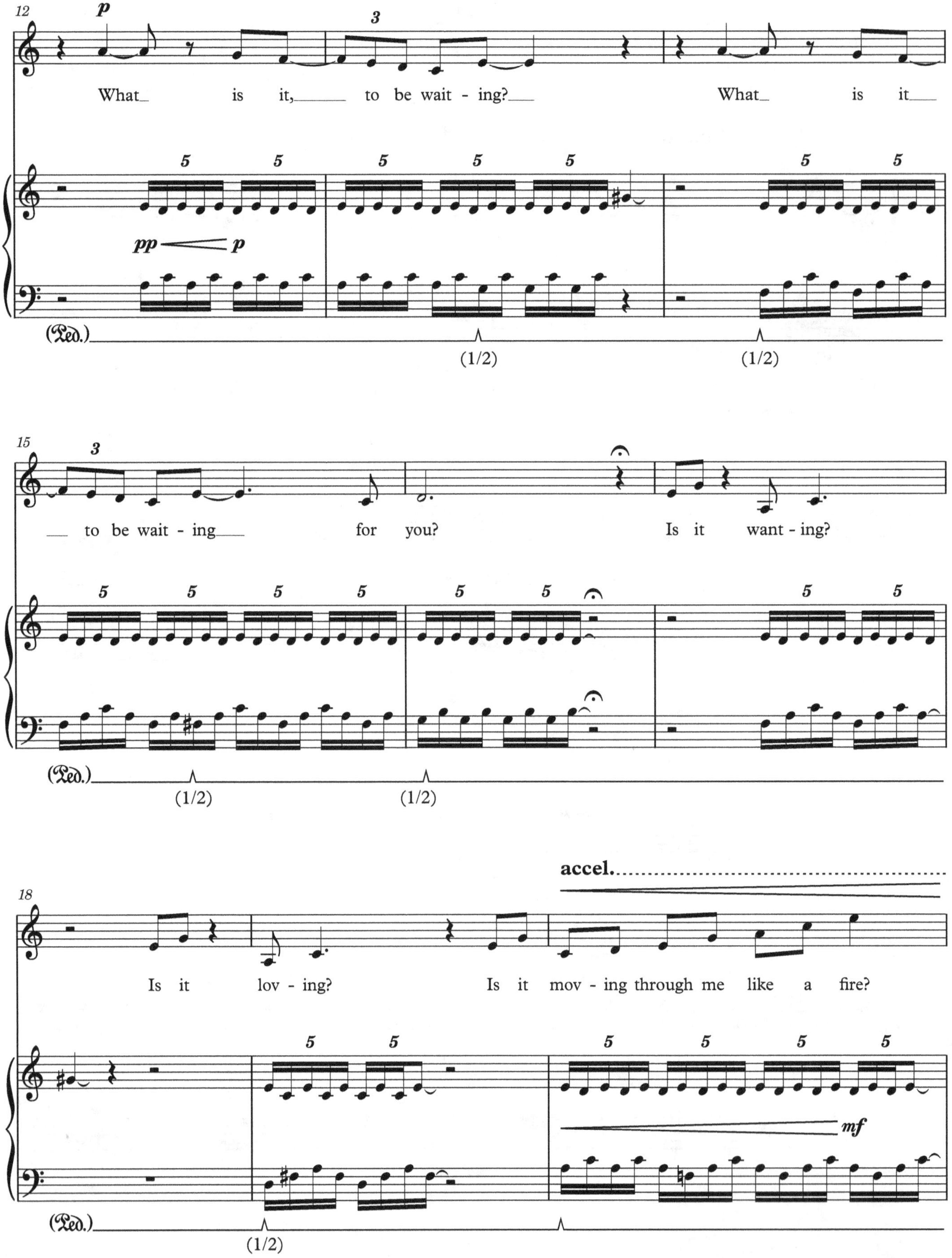

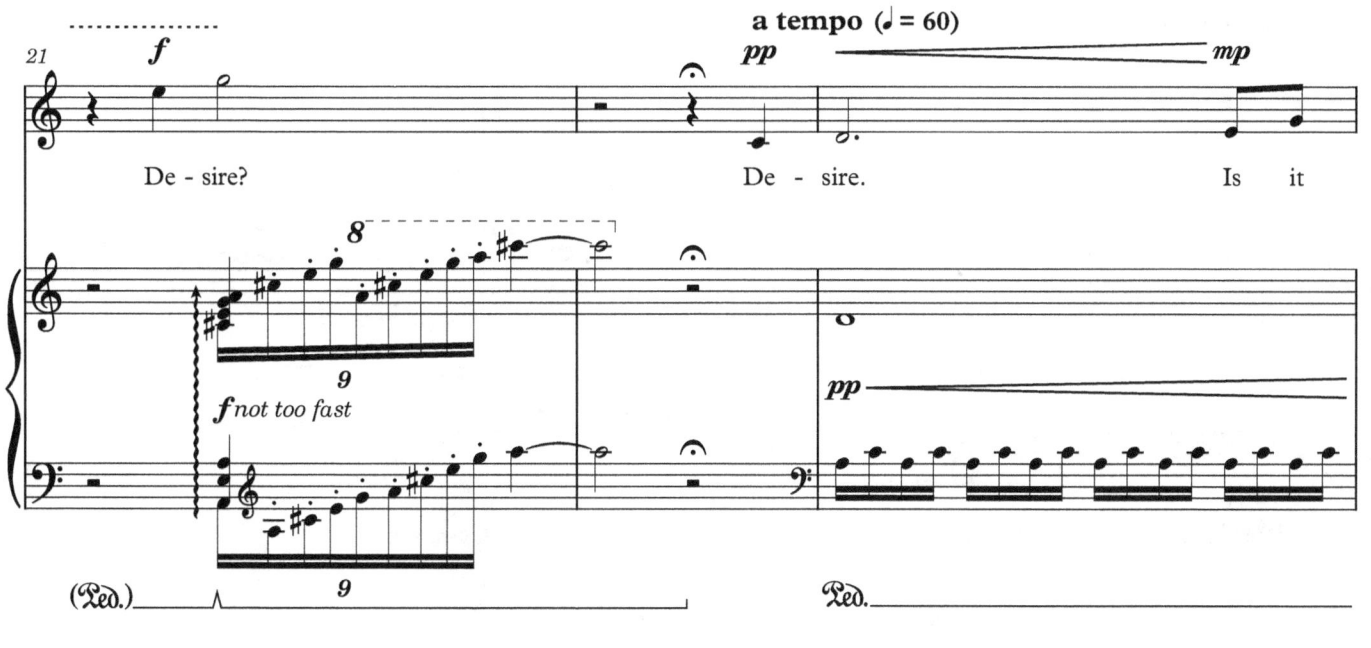

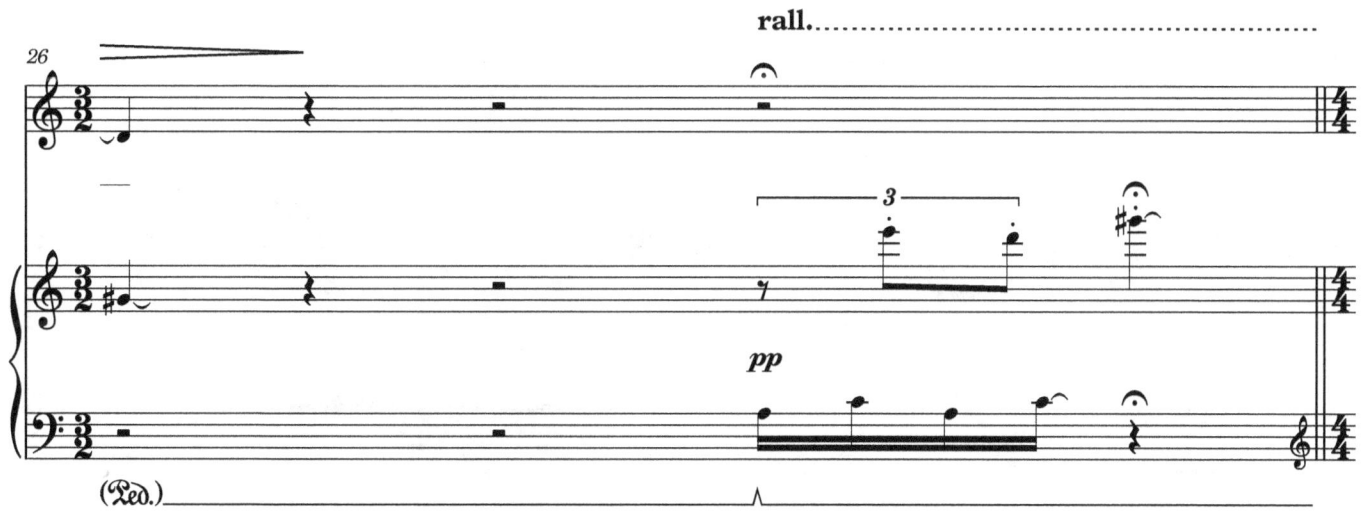

88

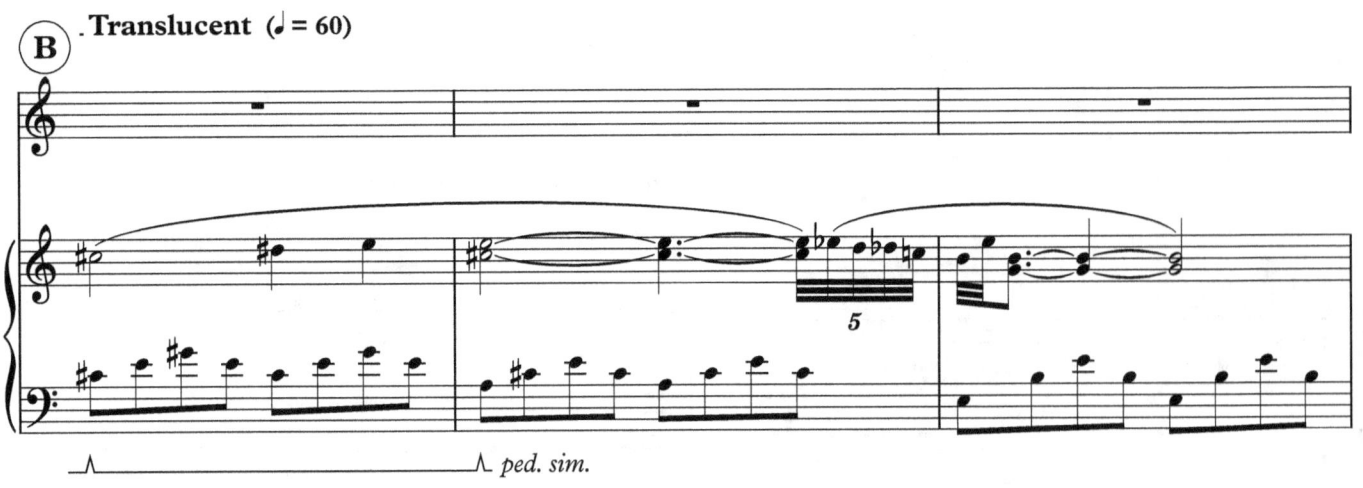
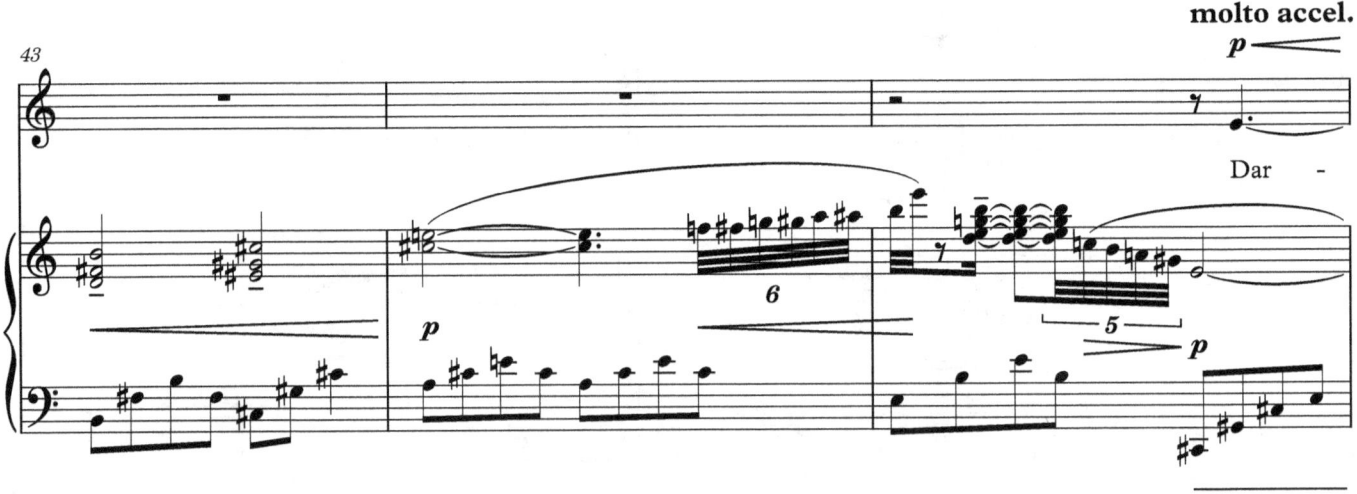

The vocal line mm. 48-66 should be sensuous and spontaneous; the "rocking back and forth" can be ad lib. as long as the harmonic changes ultimately align (the pianist should feel free to vamp or cut as necessary). Explore portamenti, glissandi, straight tone, and slow crescendi from niente on the sustained notes for an eerie, exotic effect: here Penelope, entranced, seems to weave a spell - some sort of magic to call her husband back to her.

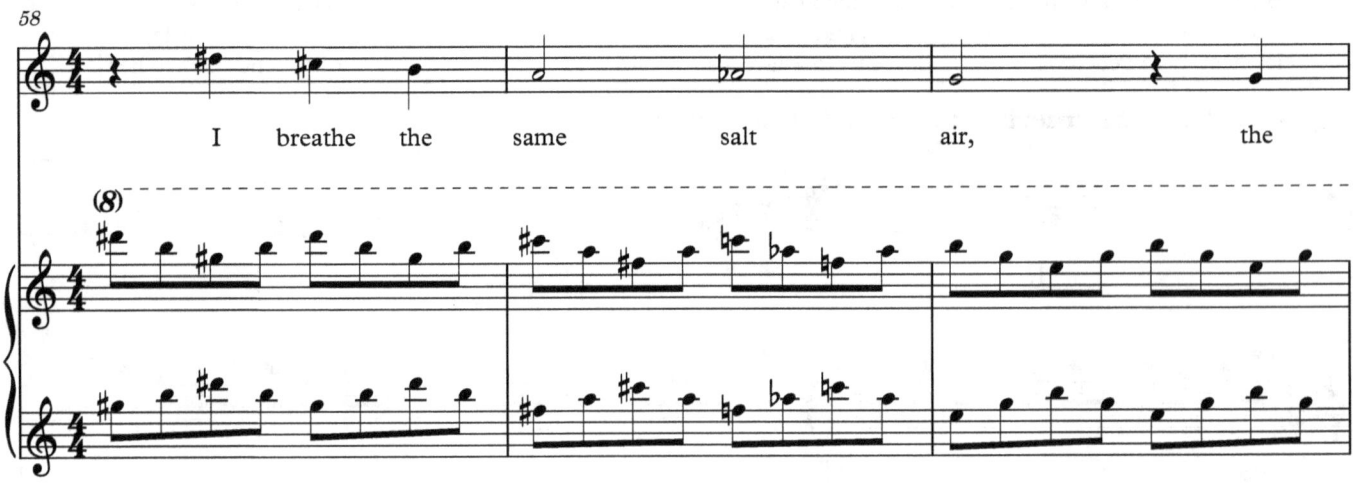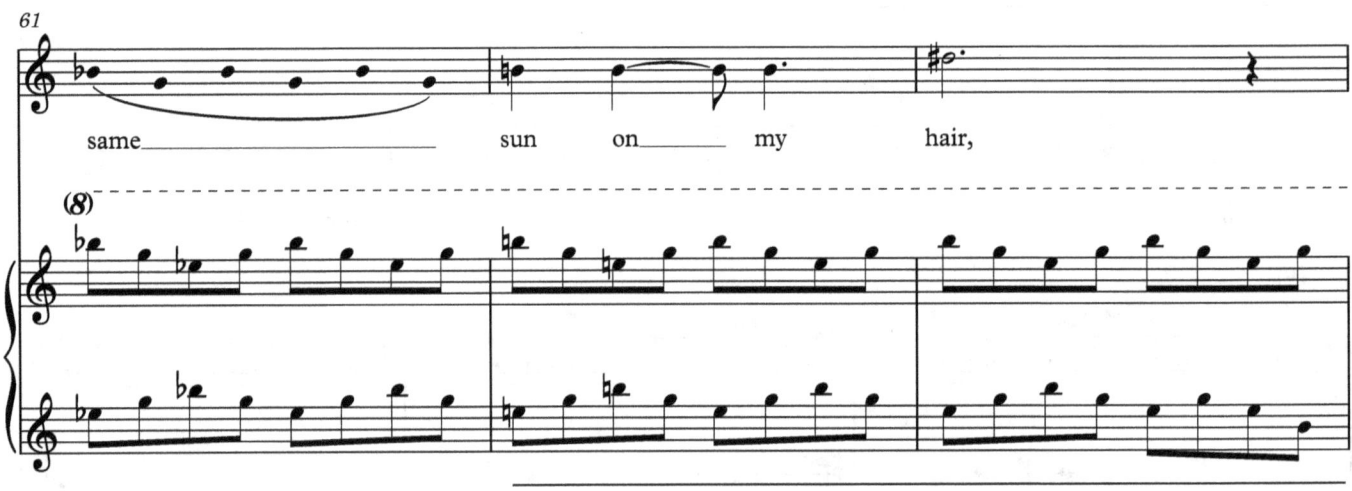

93

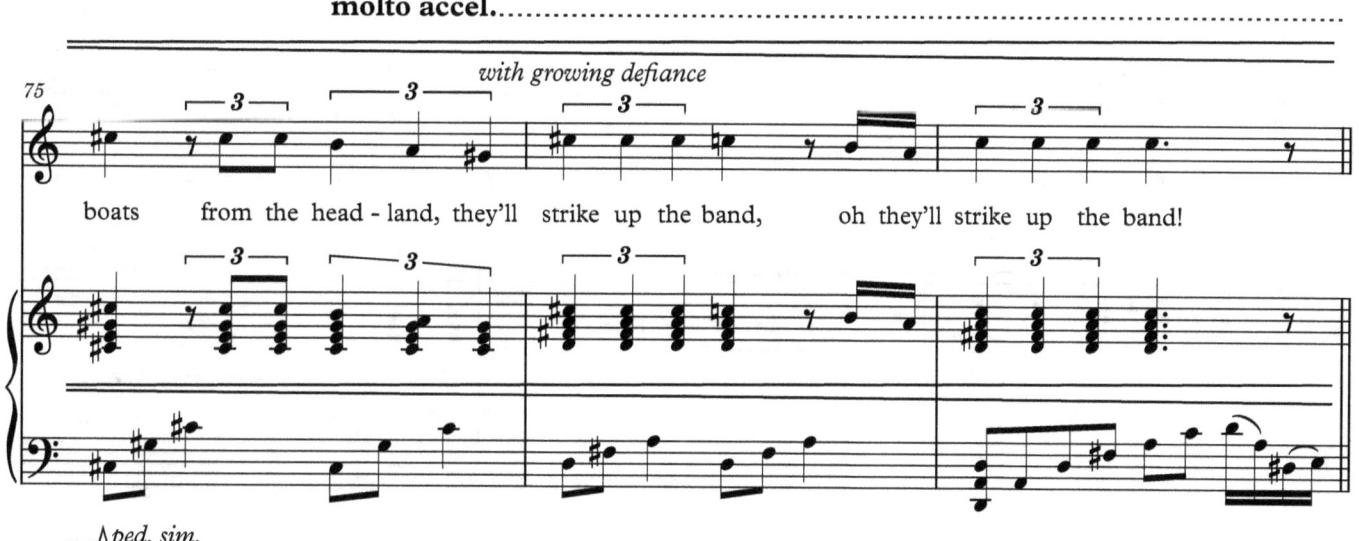

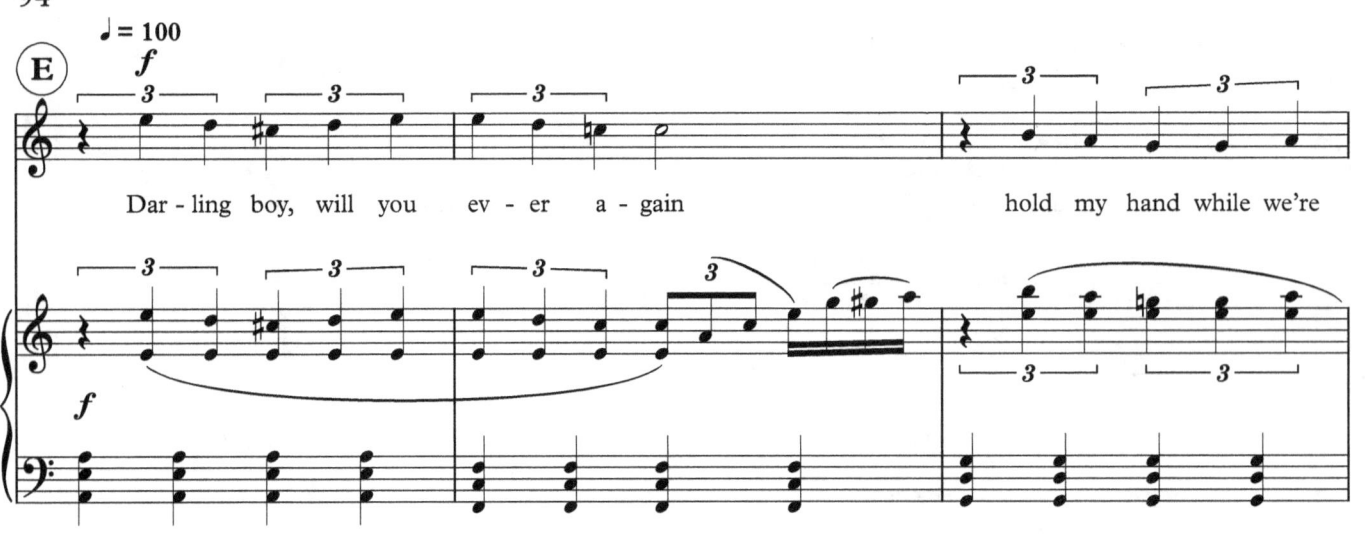

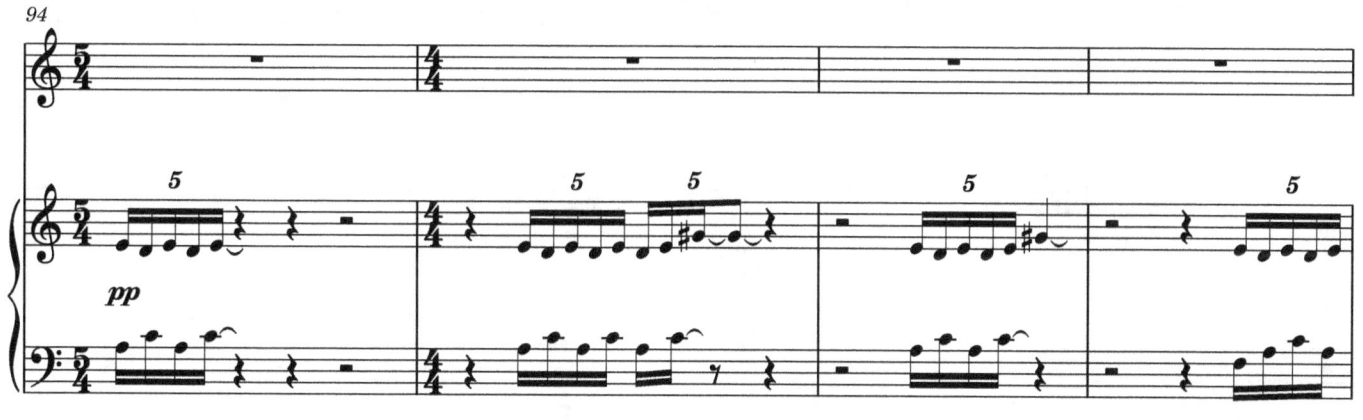

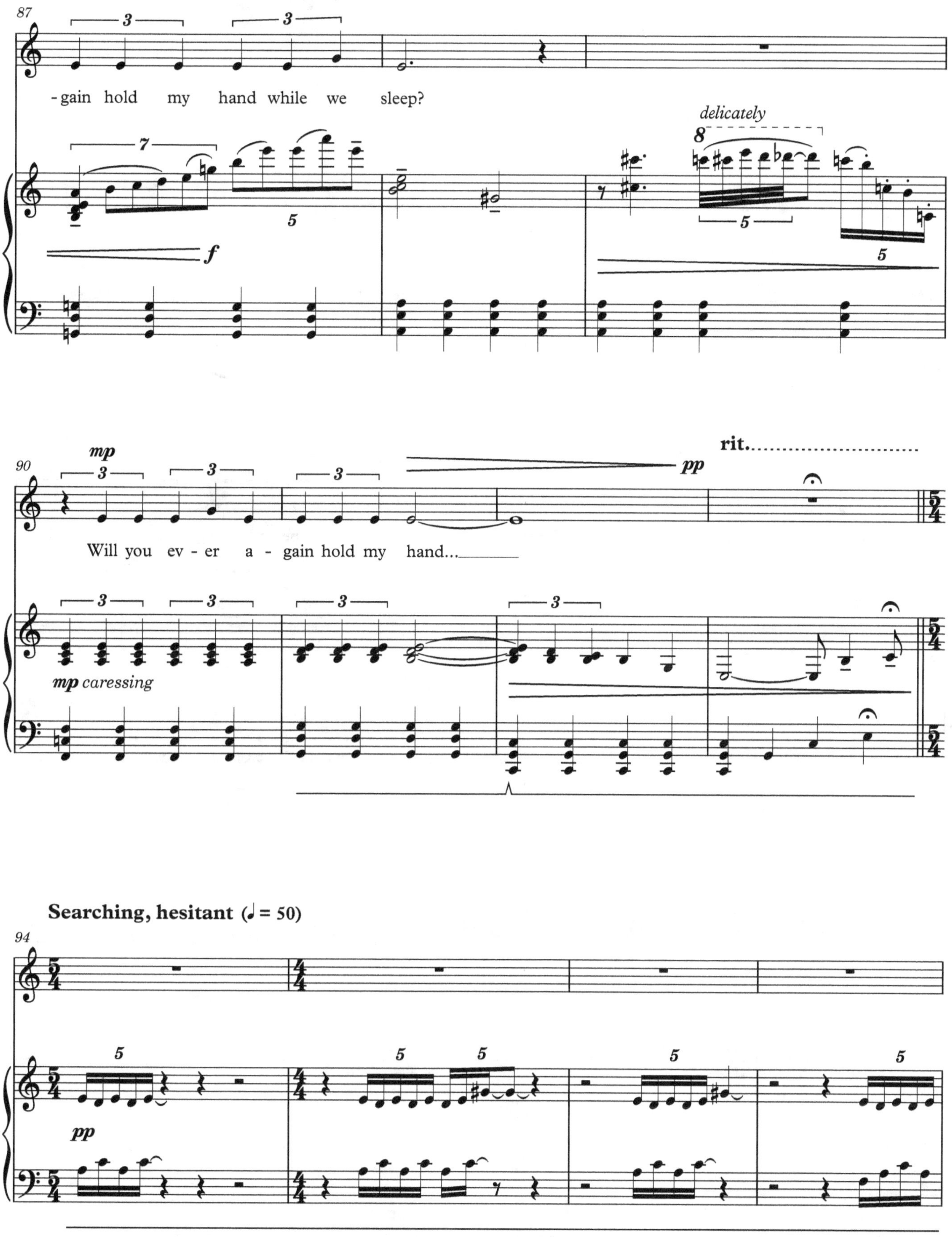
87
-gain hold my hand while we sleep?
delicately
f
90
mp
rit.
pp
Will you ev - er a - gain hold my hand...
mp caressing
Searching, hesitant (♩ = 50)
94
pp

*Written for the American Opera Projects Composers & the Voice Workshop*

# the silvery round moon

WALT WHITMAN  RAYMOND J. LUSTIG
(2008)

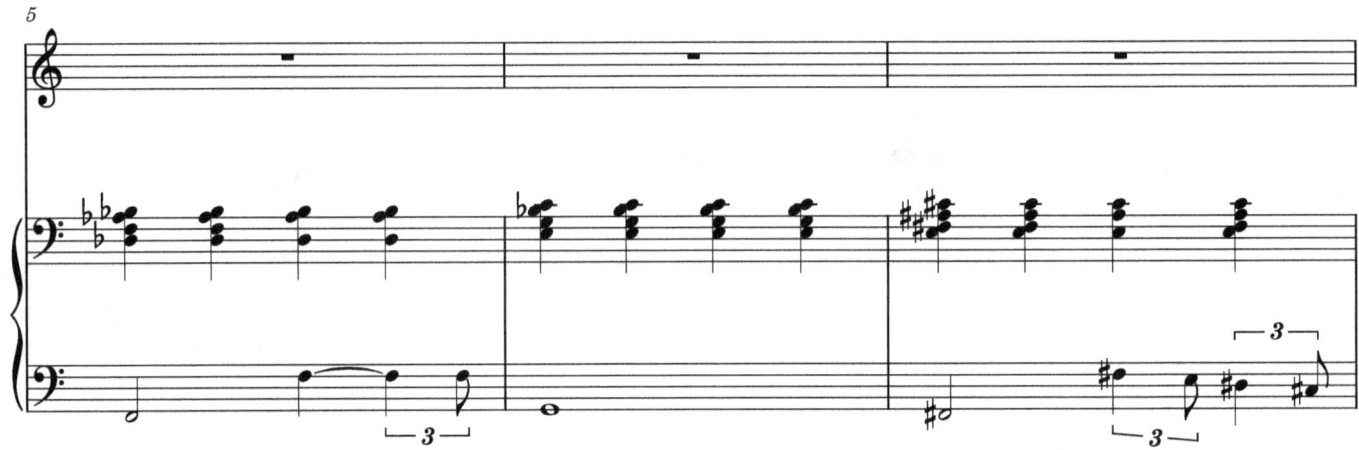

Copyright © 2008 by Raymond J. Lustig Music. All Rights Reserved.

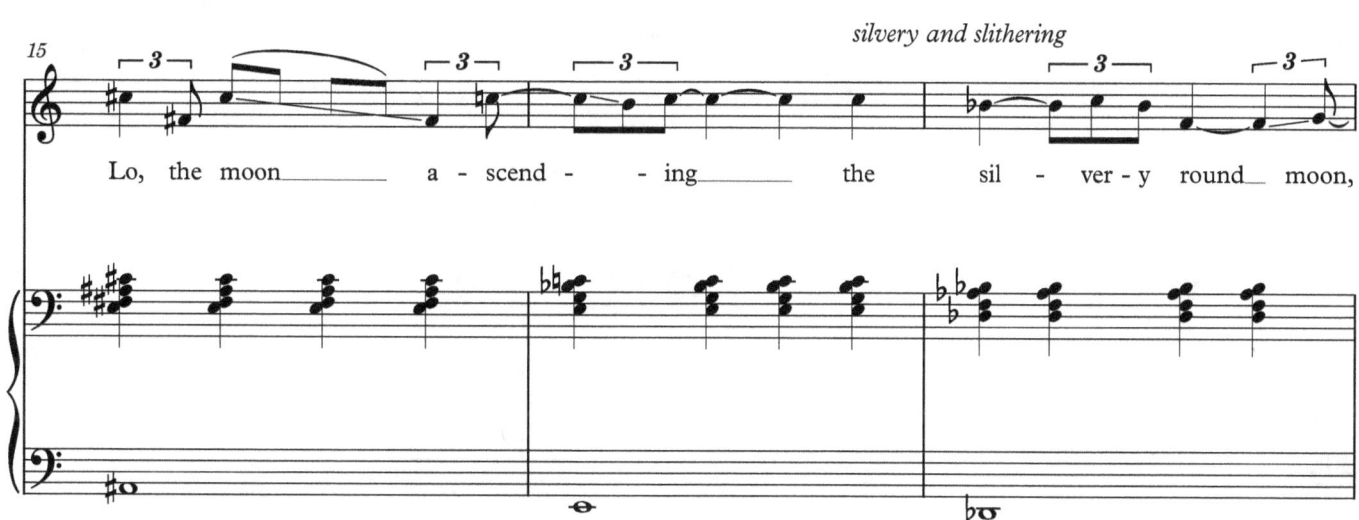
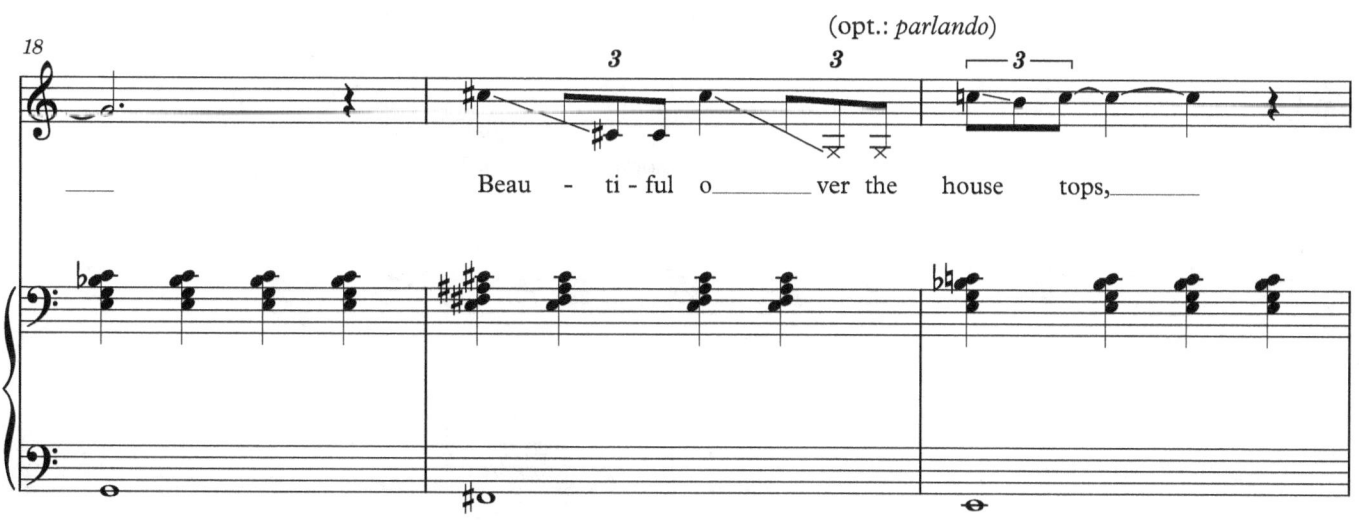

100

\* humming or "ooh"-ing dreamily, with eerie glissand and tight, narrow vibrato
\*\* slow, languid glissando

31
Up from the east
mp
the sil - ver - y round
35
moon,
Beau - ti - ful o - ver the
house - tops,
like weird vibrato
39
mf
ghast - - ly, phan - tom
moon
* slow, languid glissando

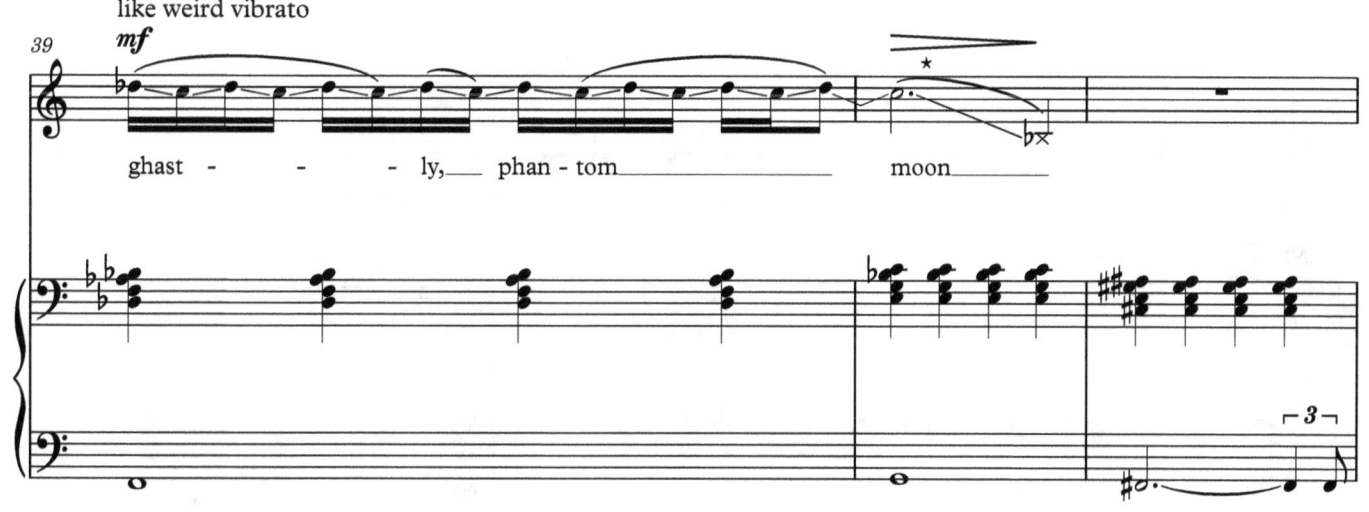

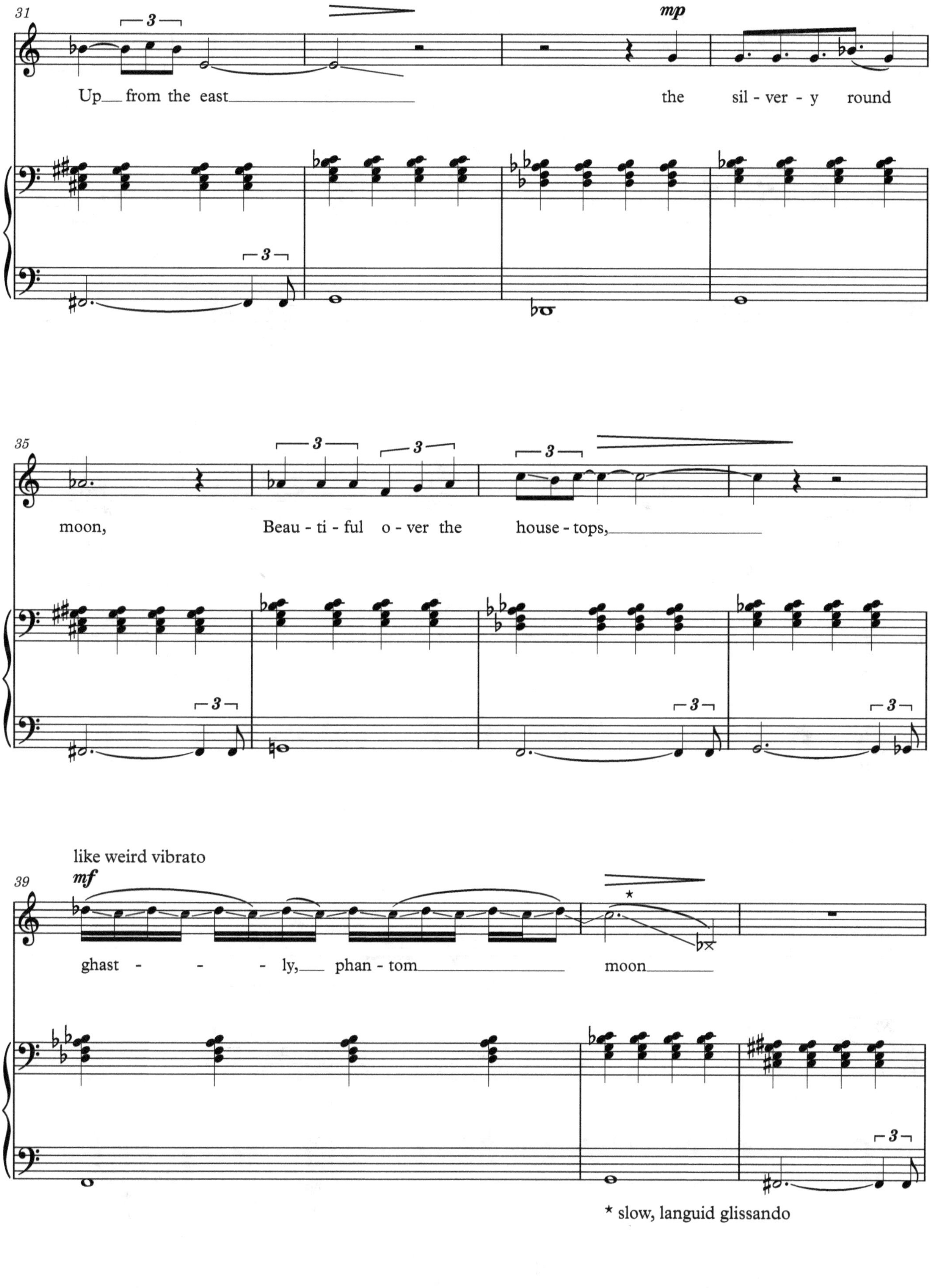

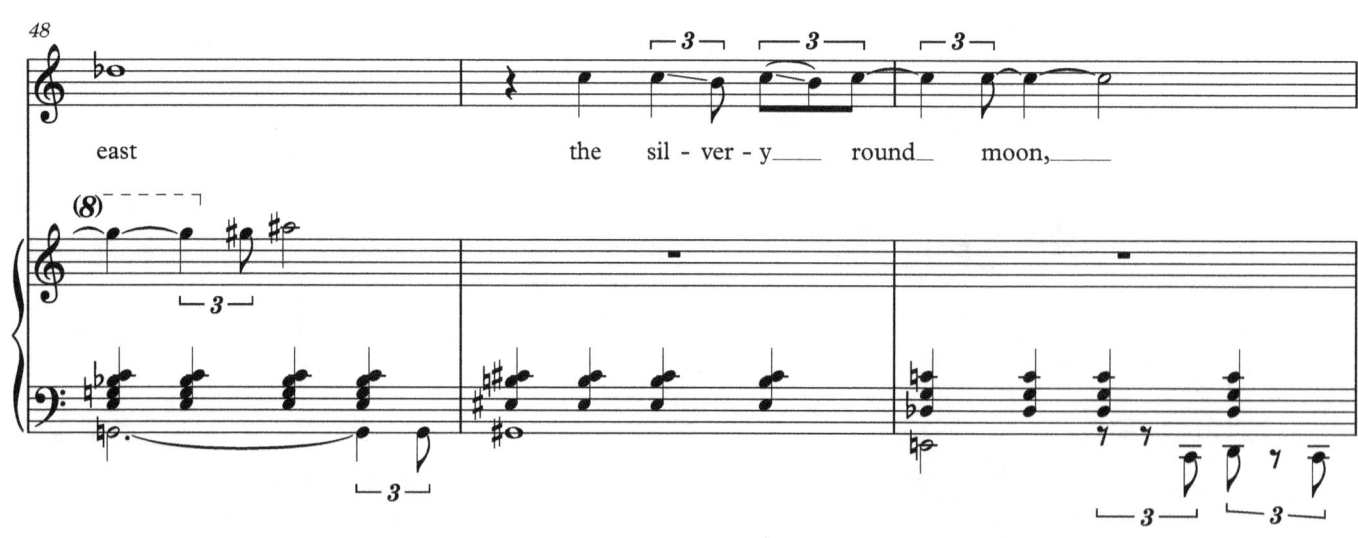

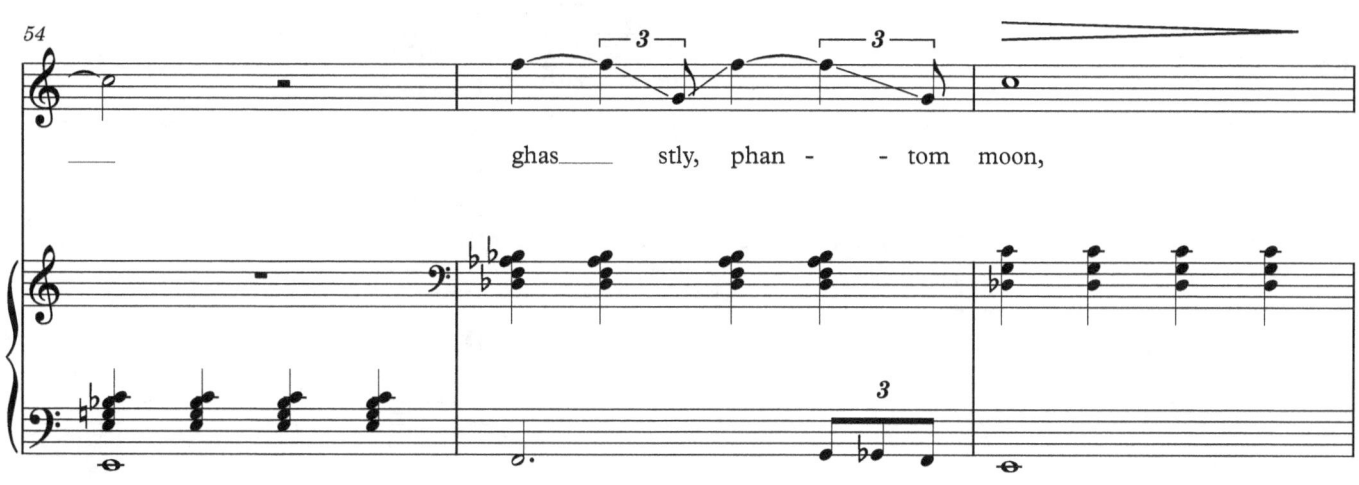

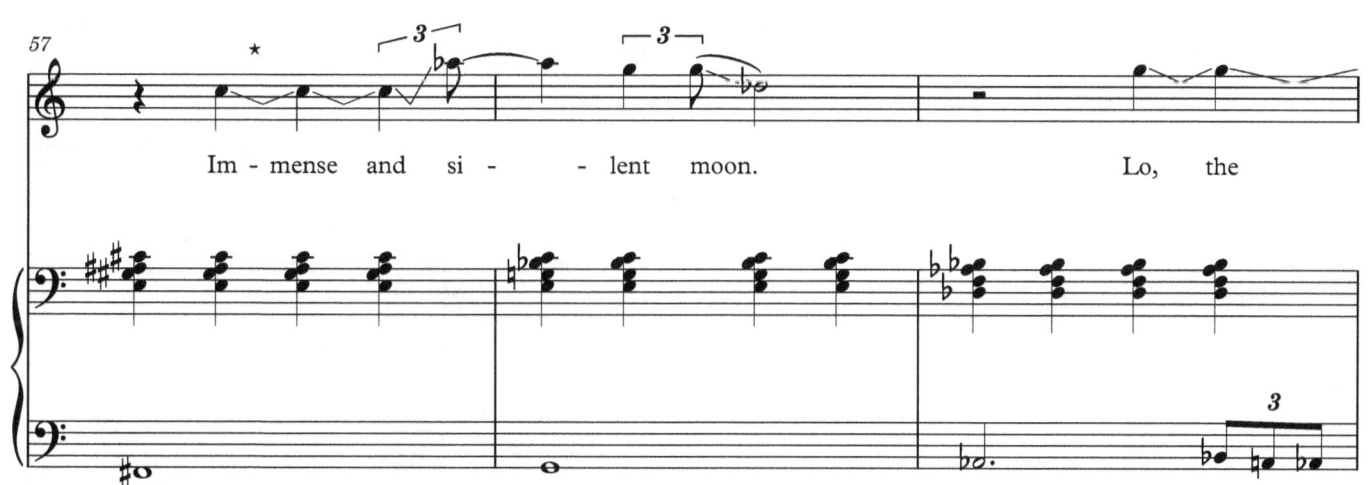

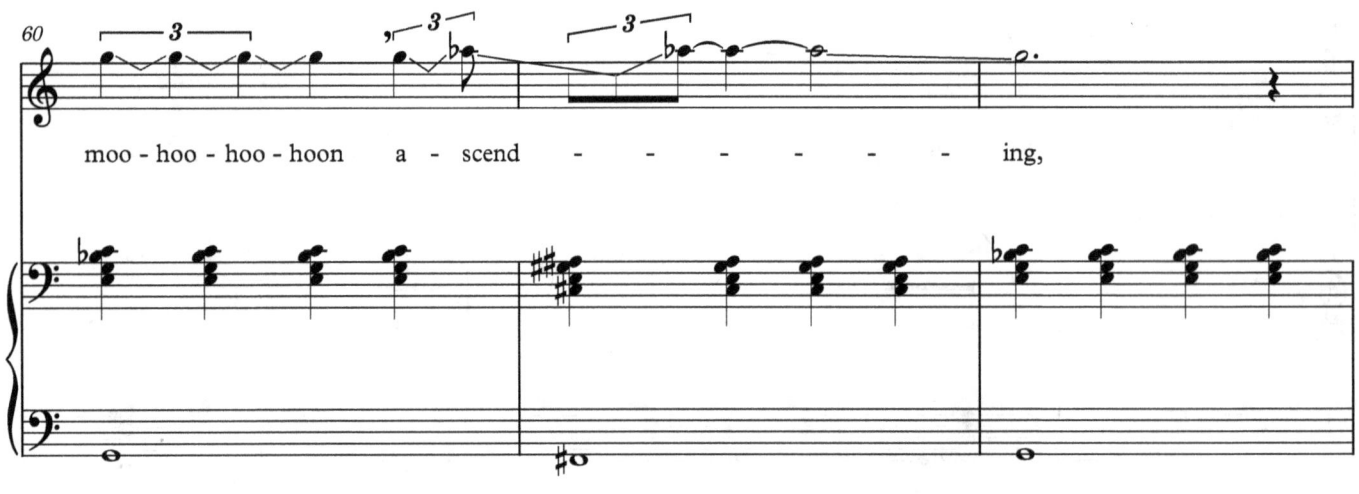

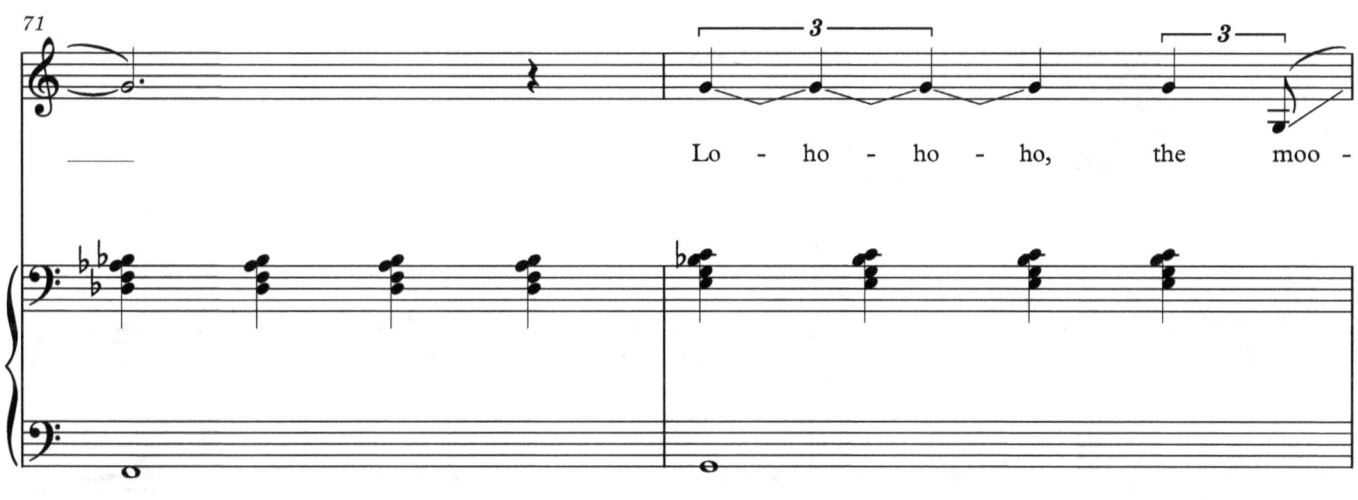
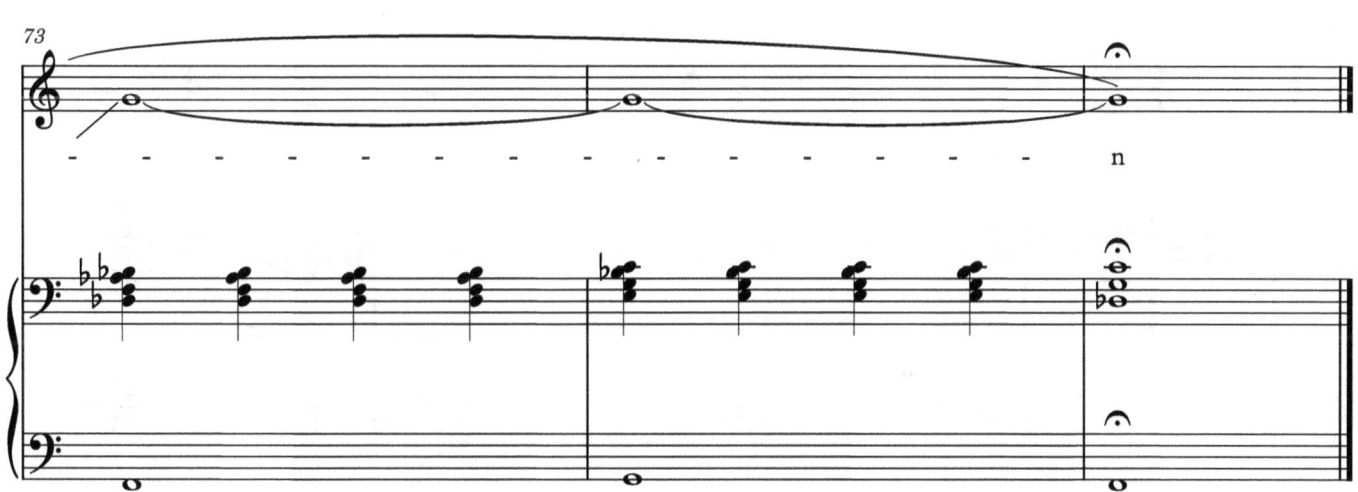

# Be Music, Night

KENNETH PATCHEN

CARRIE MAGIN
(2011)

Copyright © 2011 by Two Places Publishing (ASCAP). All Rights Reserved.
Text copyright © by Kenneth Patchen. Used with the kind permission of the author.

108

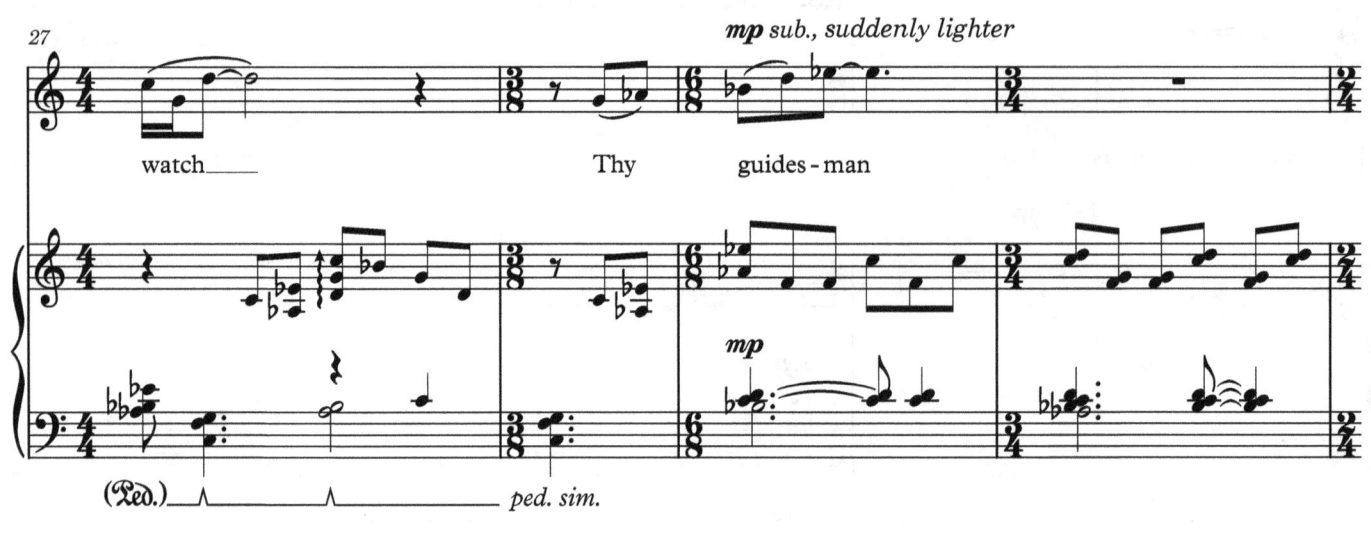

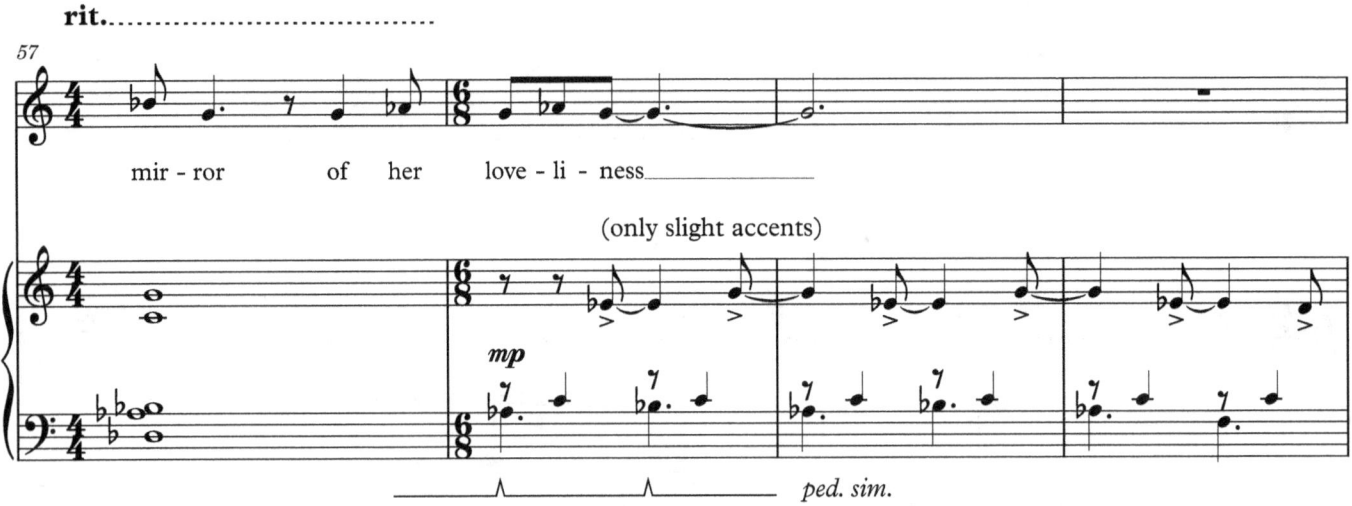

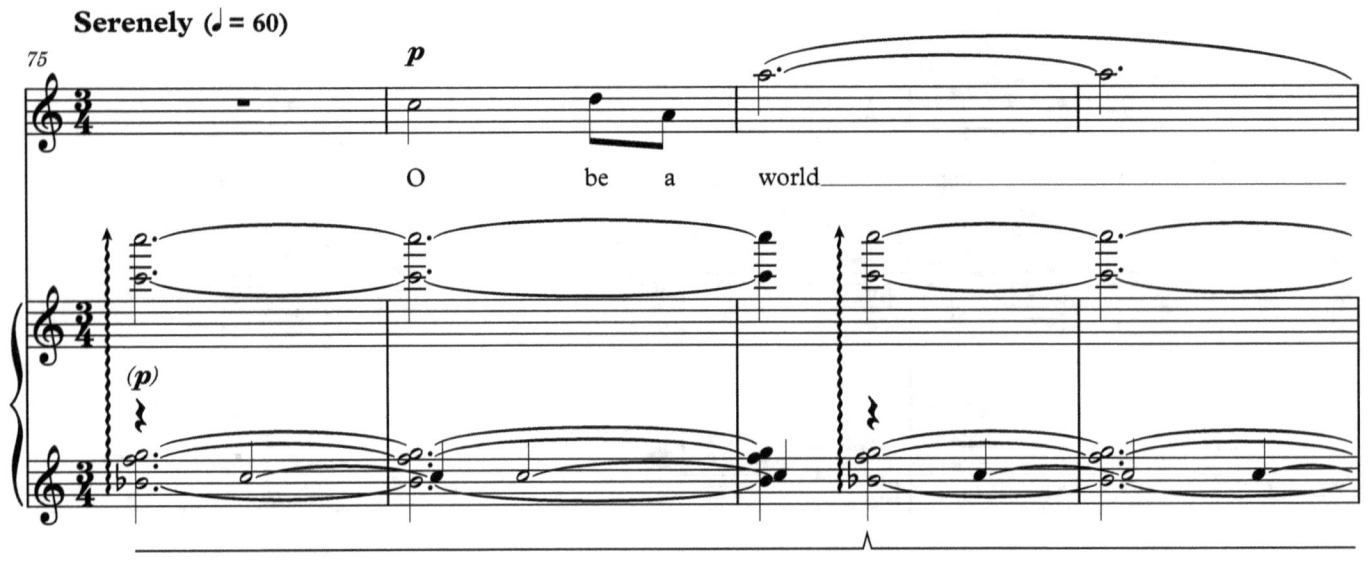
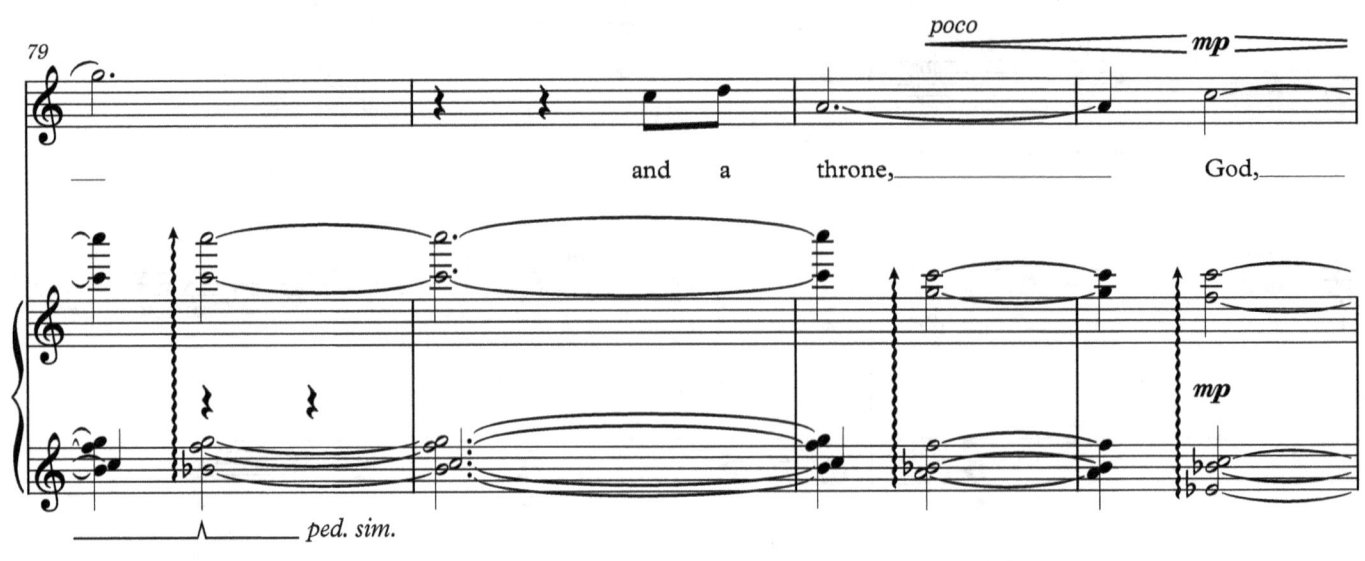
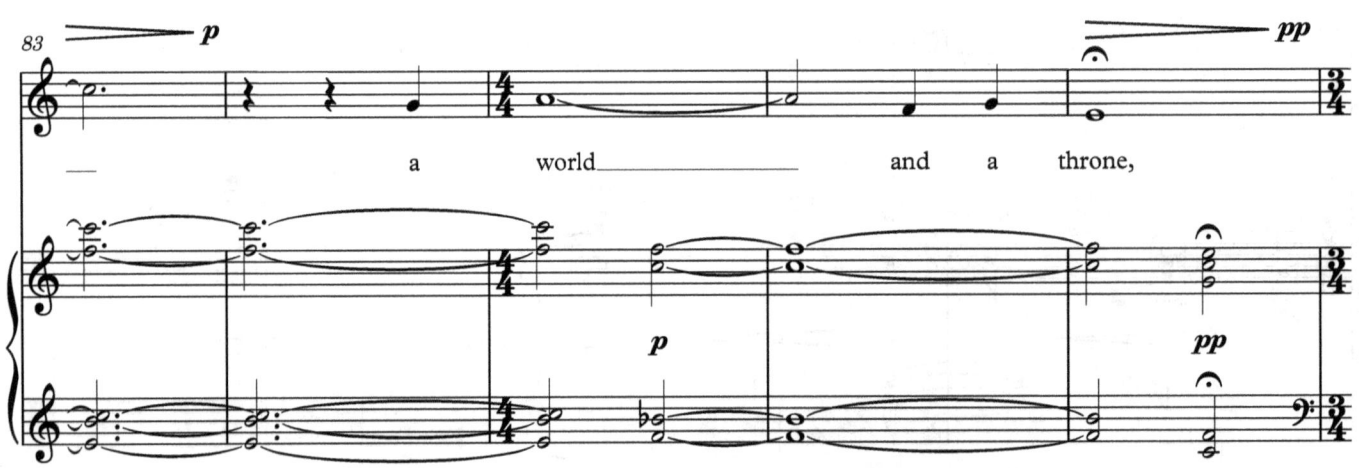

114

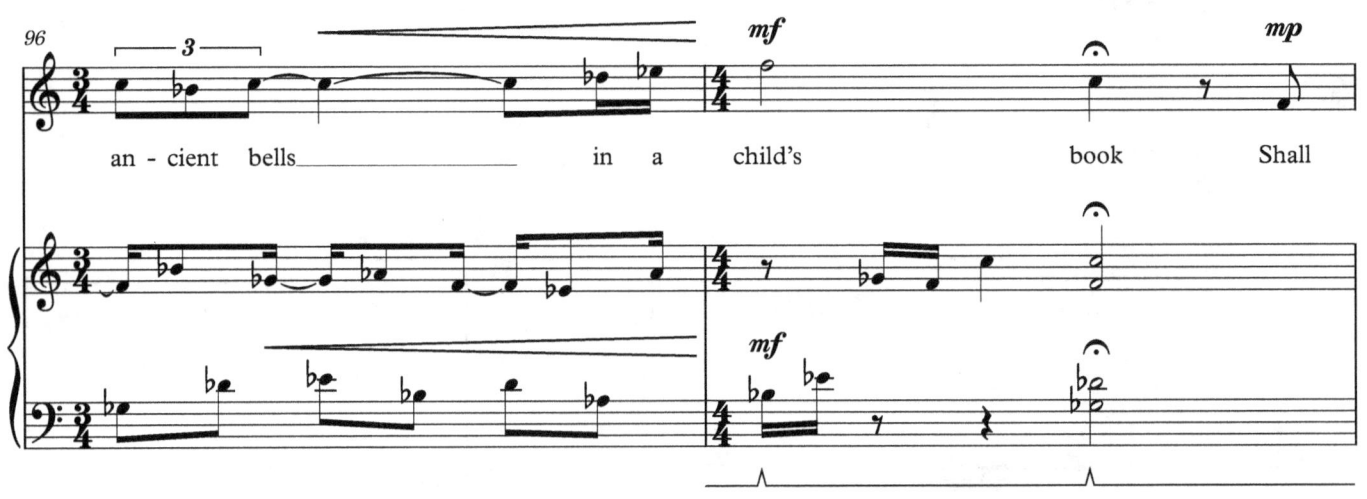

fields_____ en - ti - re - ly fold - ed in -

-side the glass bell__ of rain and

117

sun - - light.    I

woke_____ up.

What    is    cloud - - - ing    the

119

# Every Day is a God
*from Holy the Firm*

ANNIE DILLARD

JAMES PRIMOSCH
(2012)

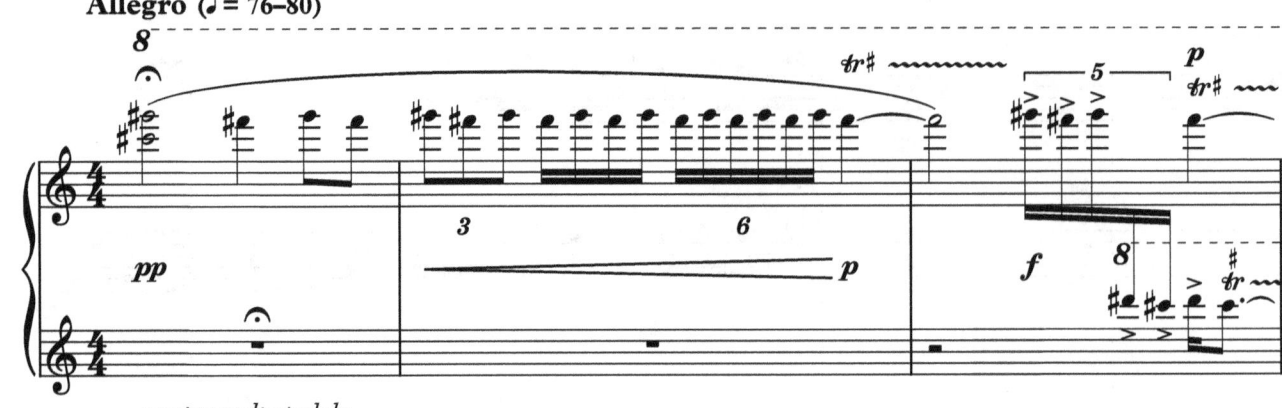
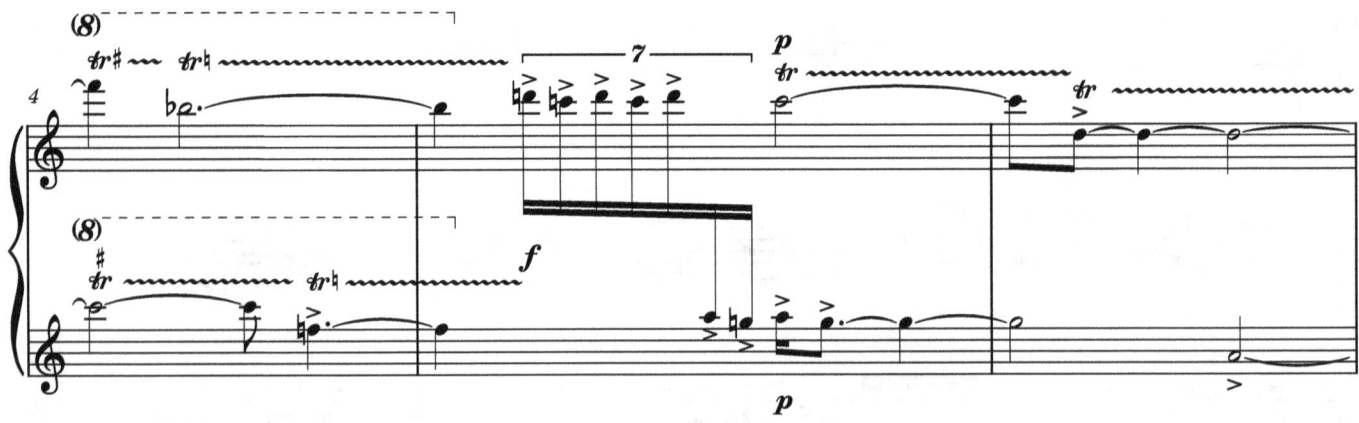

Copyright © 2013 by Merion Music, Inc. Teodore Presser Co., Sole Representative.
All Rights Reserved. International Copyright Secured.
Text from Holy the Firm by Annie Dillard. Copyright © 1977 by Annie Dillard.

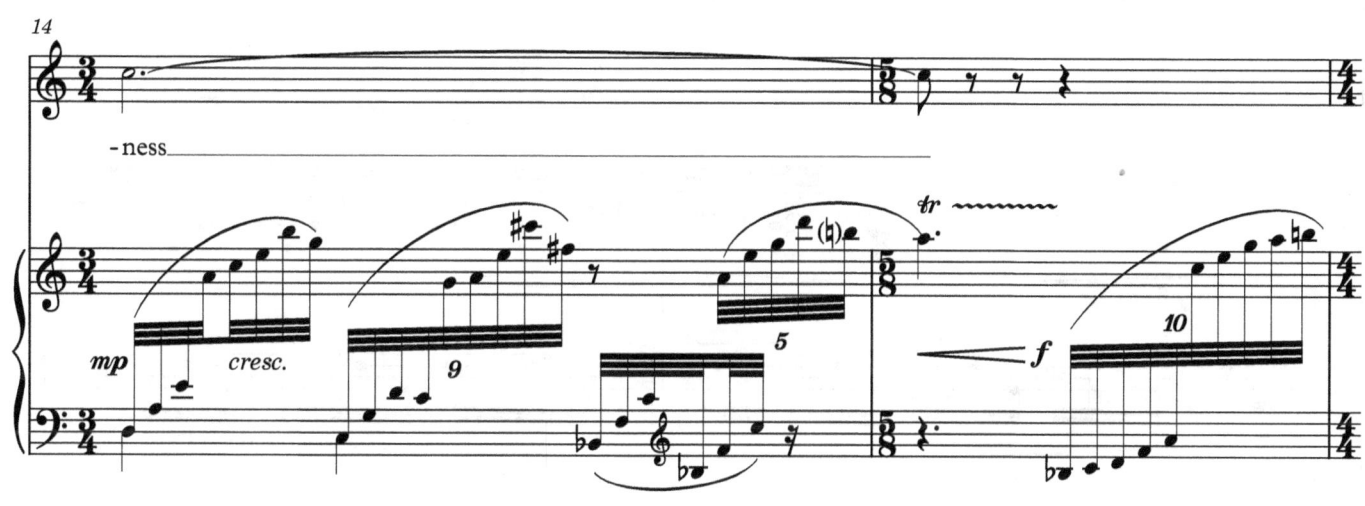

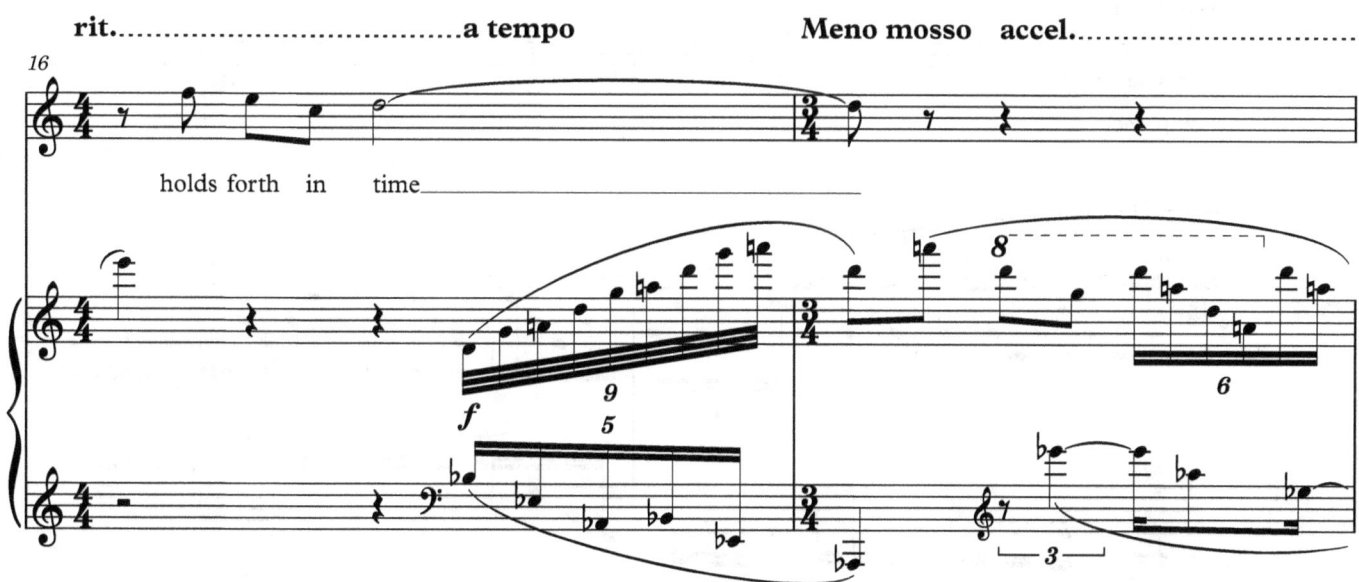

a tempo
18
6
6
6
3
tr♯
10
f
3
20
mf
I
tr♯
p
6
6
6
mp
p
22
3
wor - ship each god,
I
praise
each
day
6
6
6
6
6
6
6
6

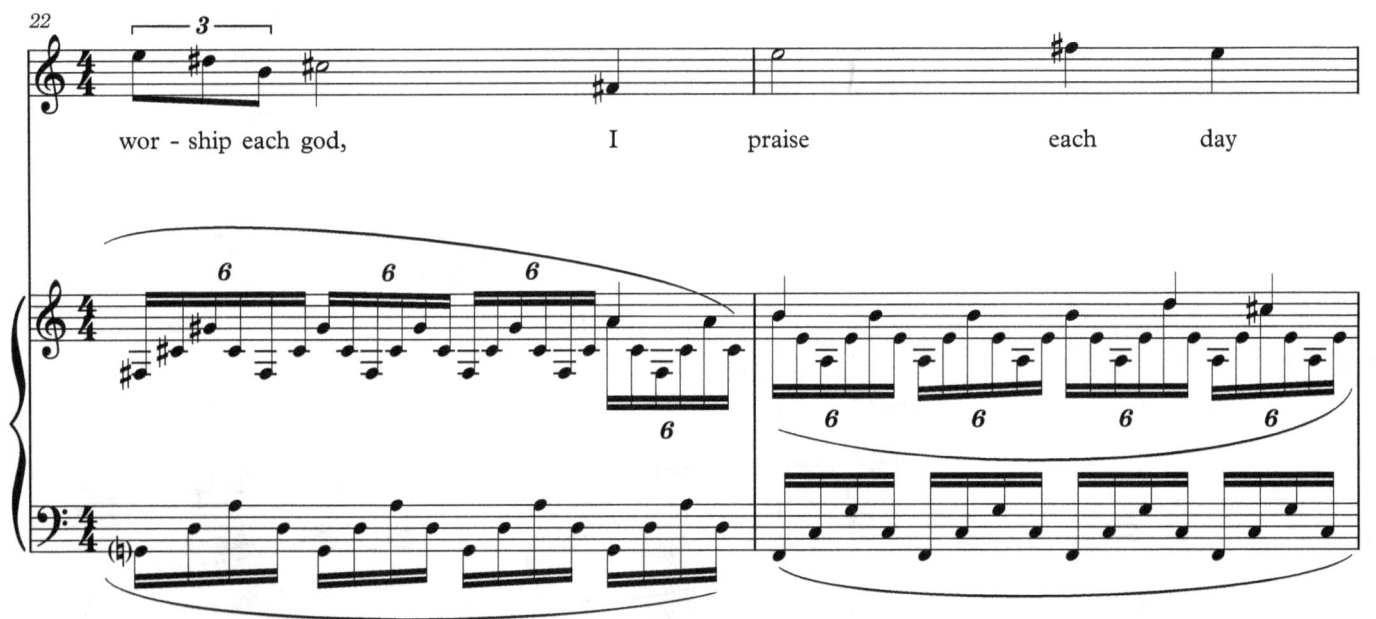

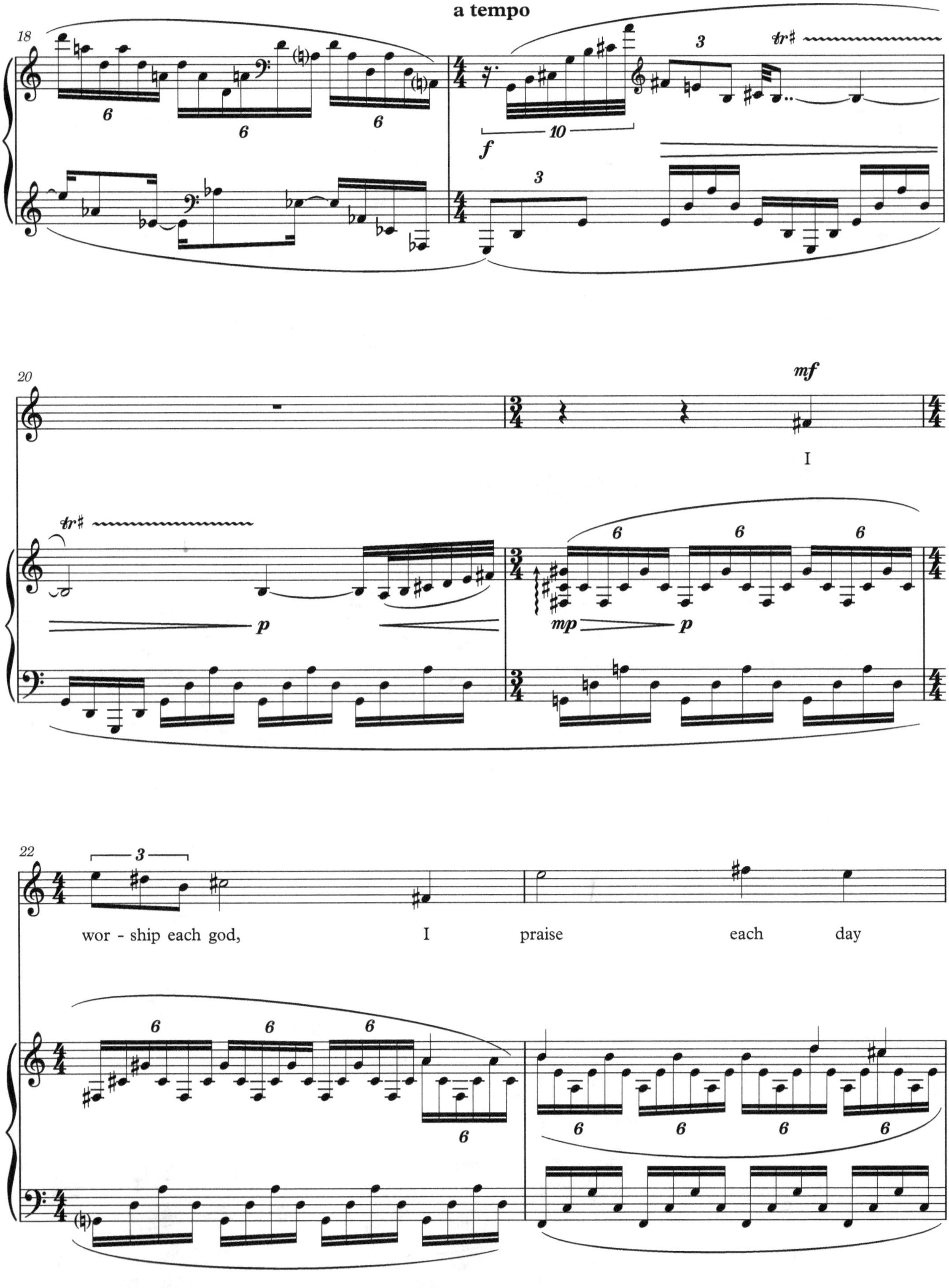

128

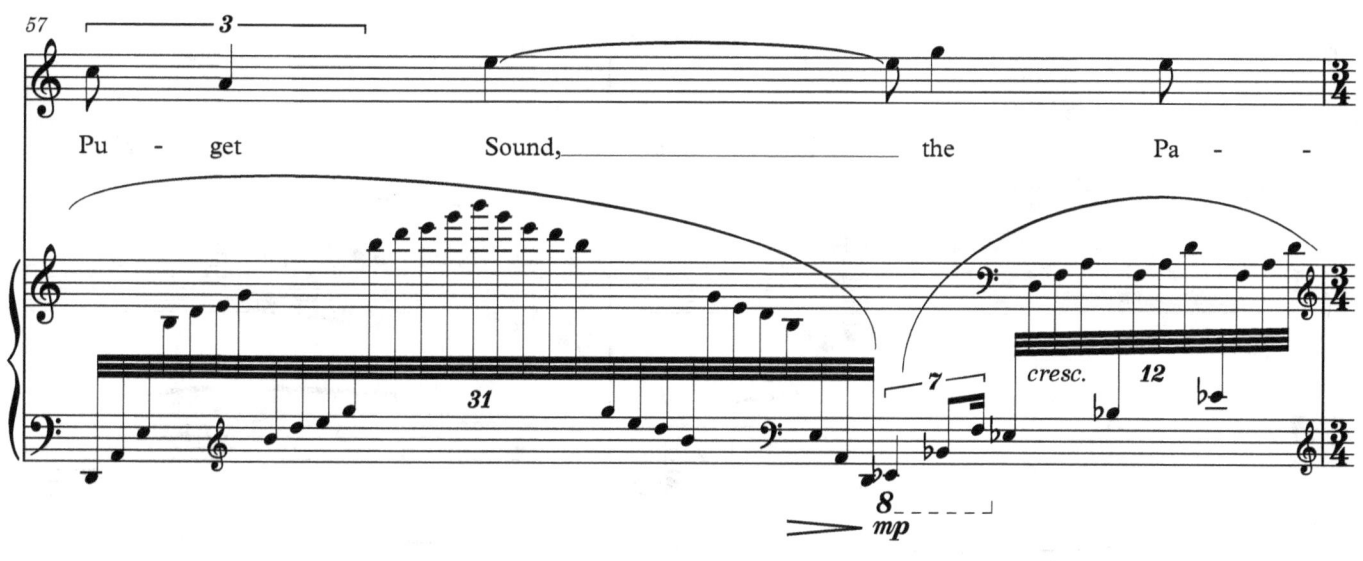
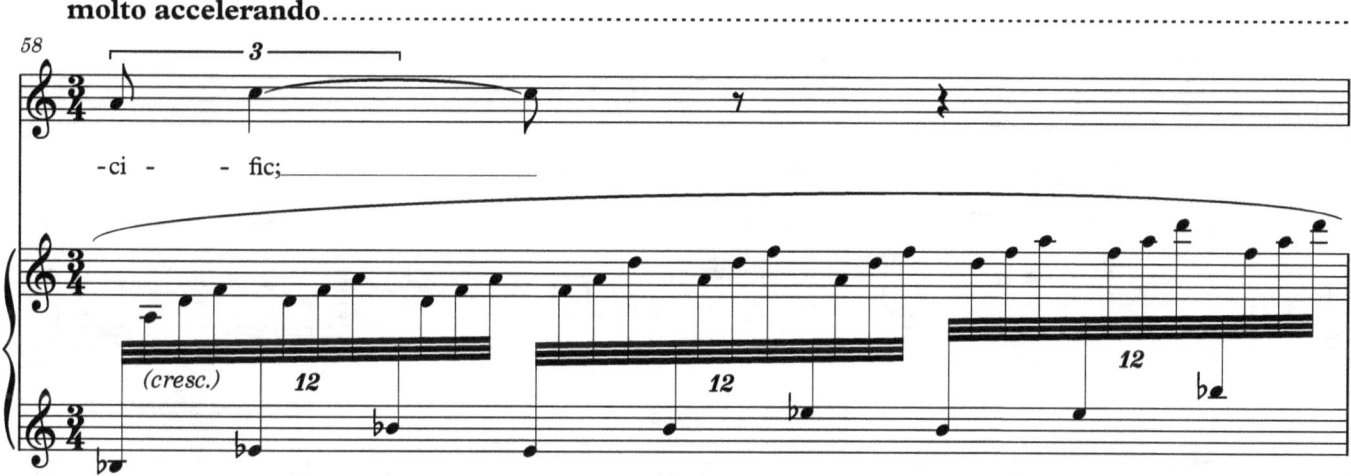
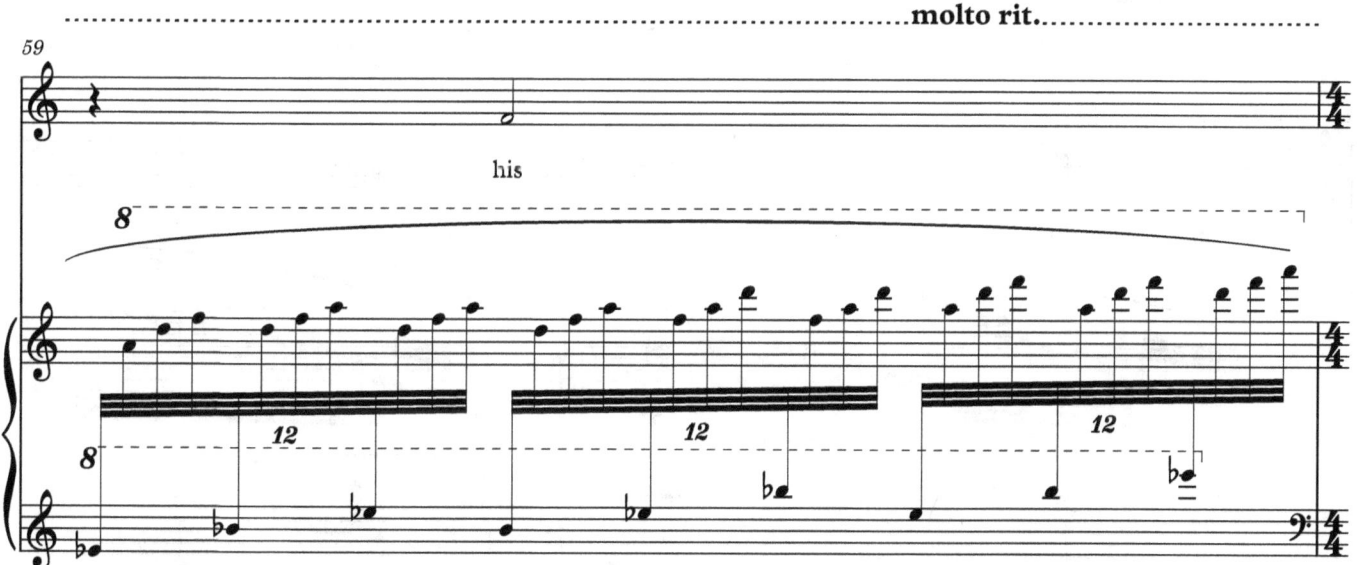

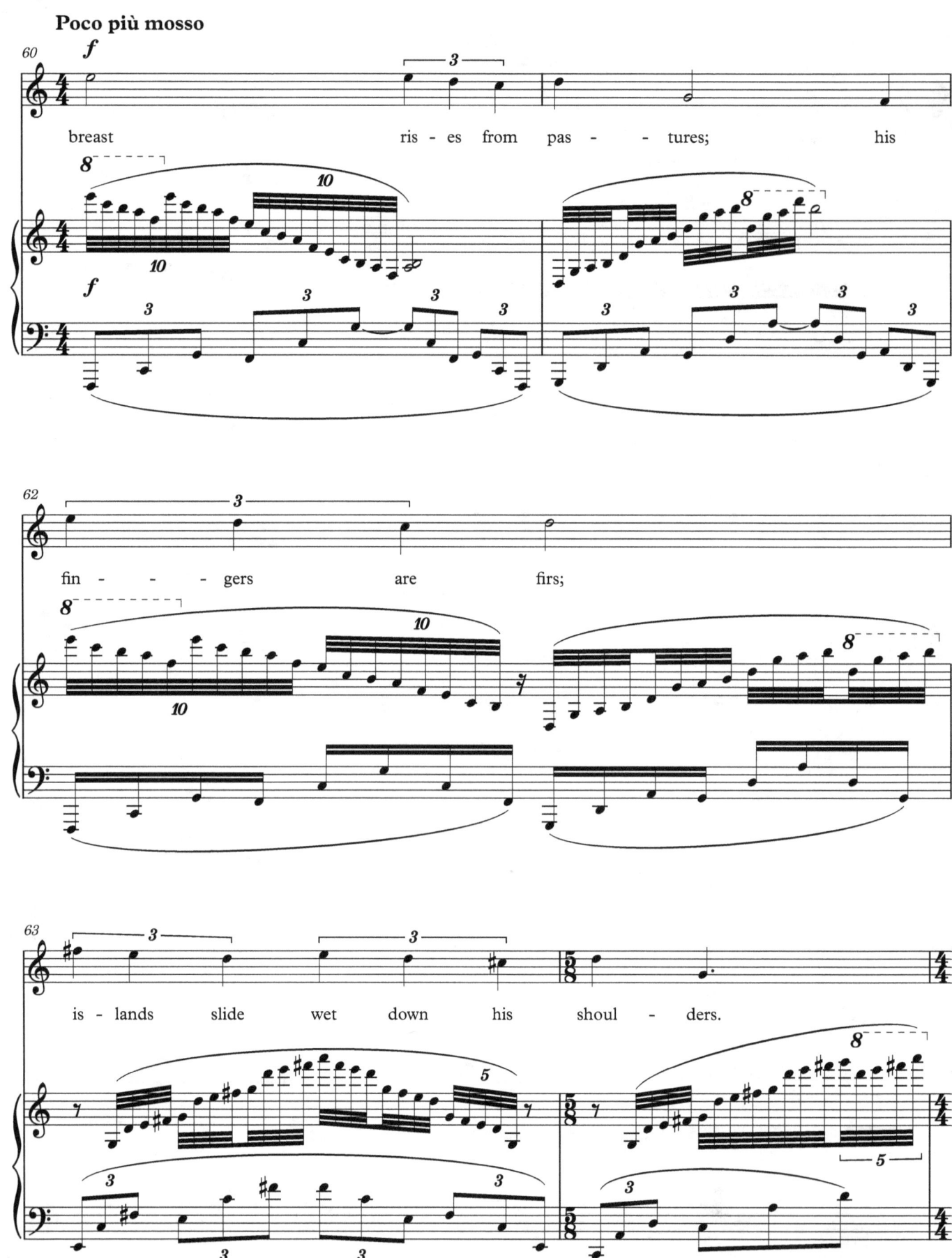

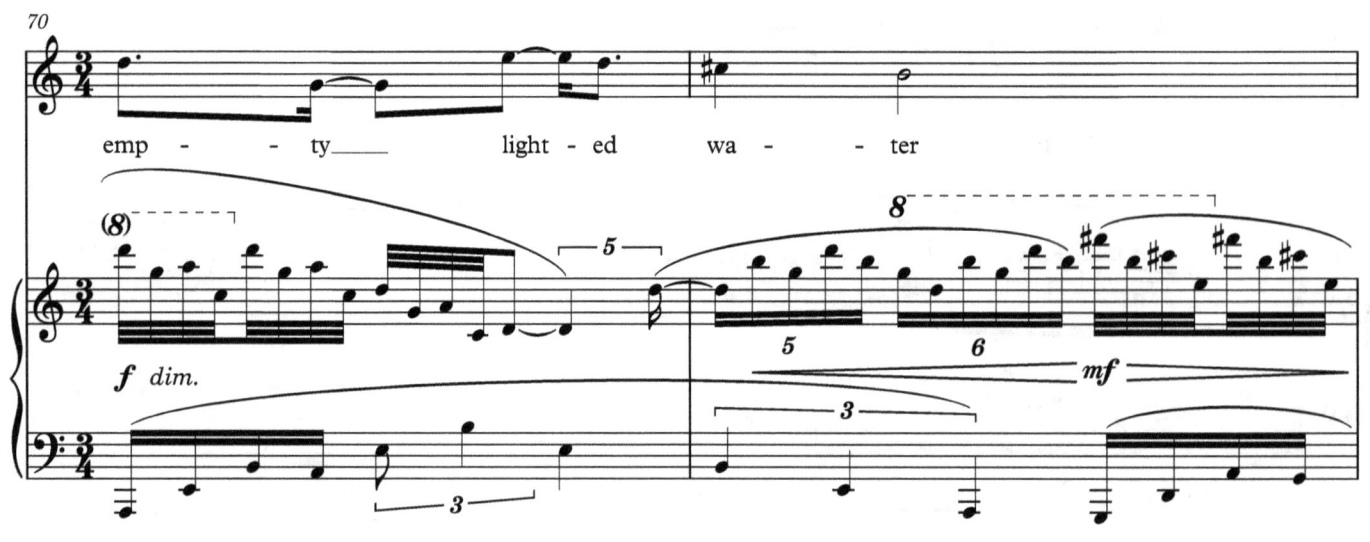
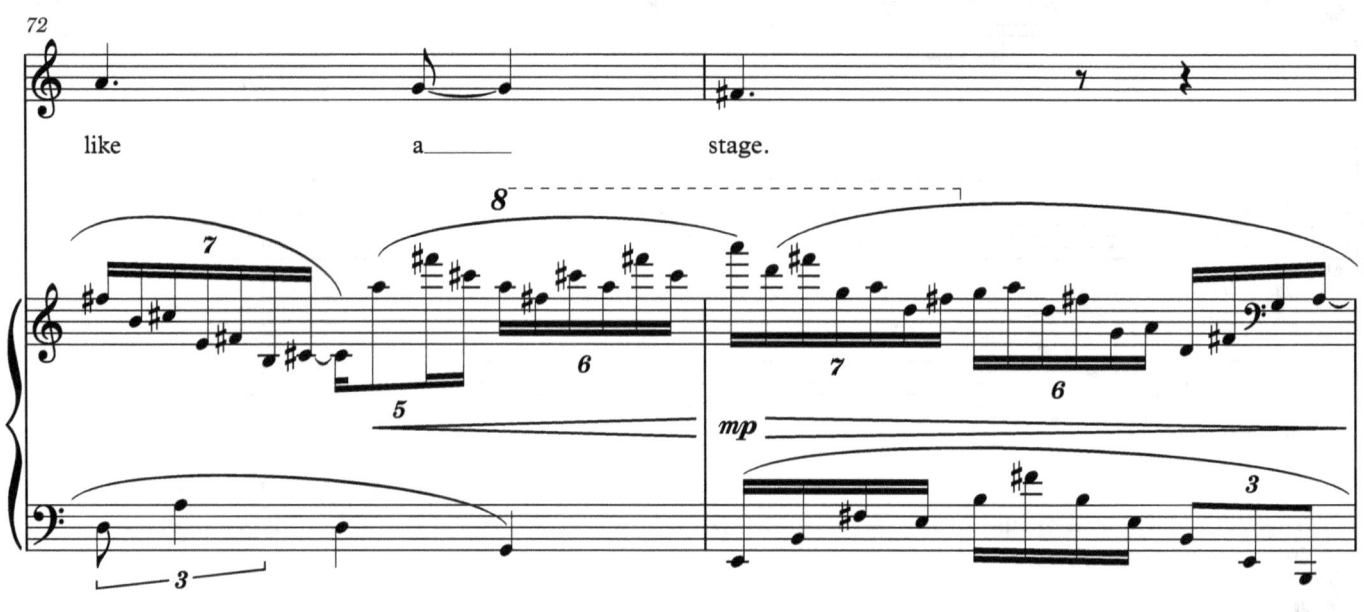
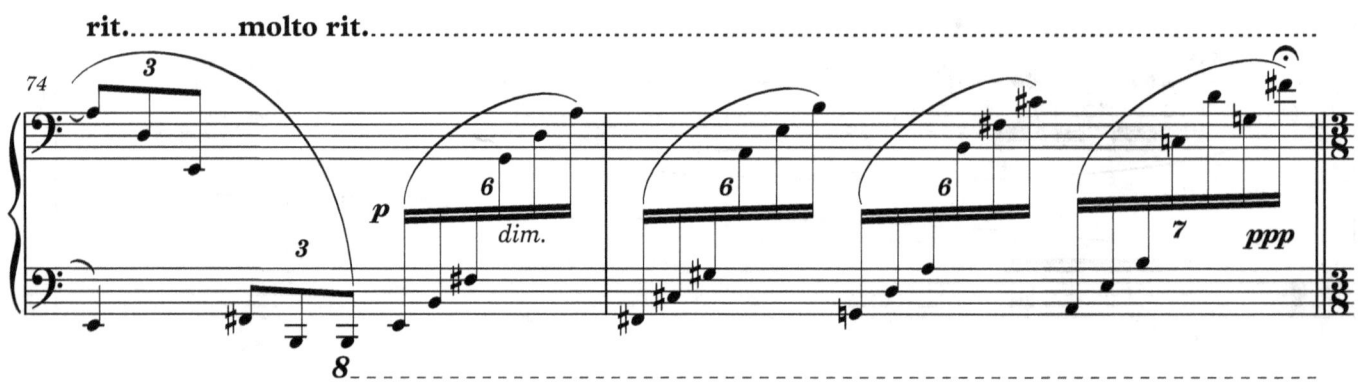

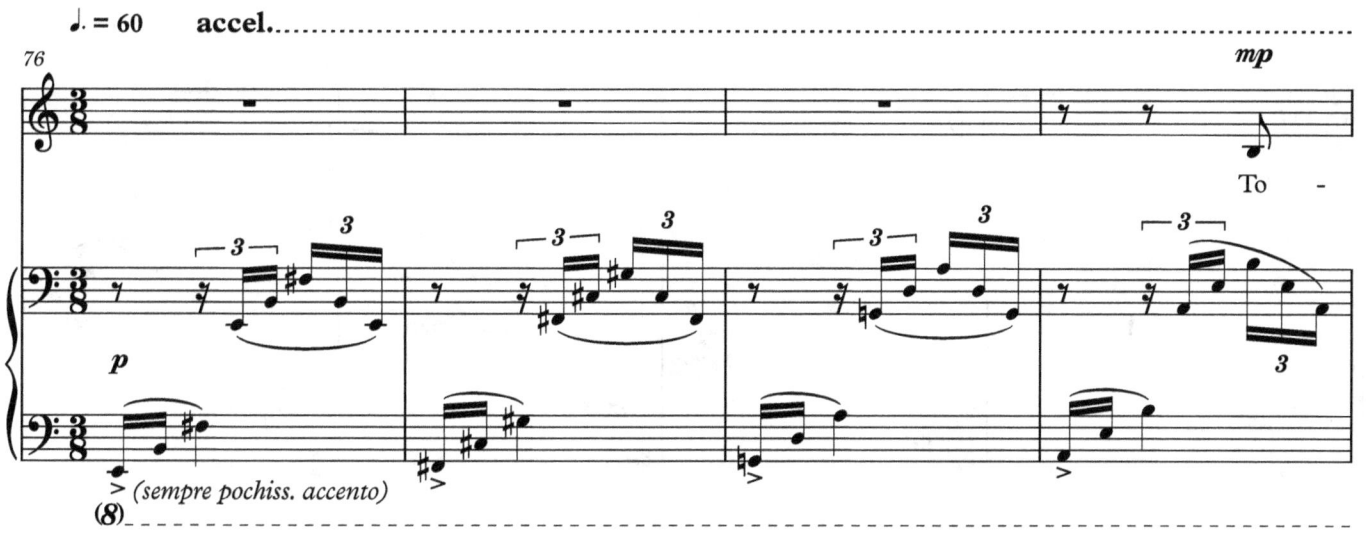
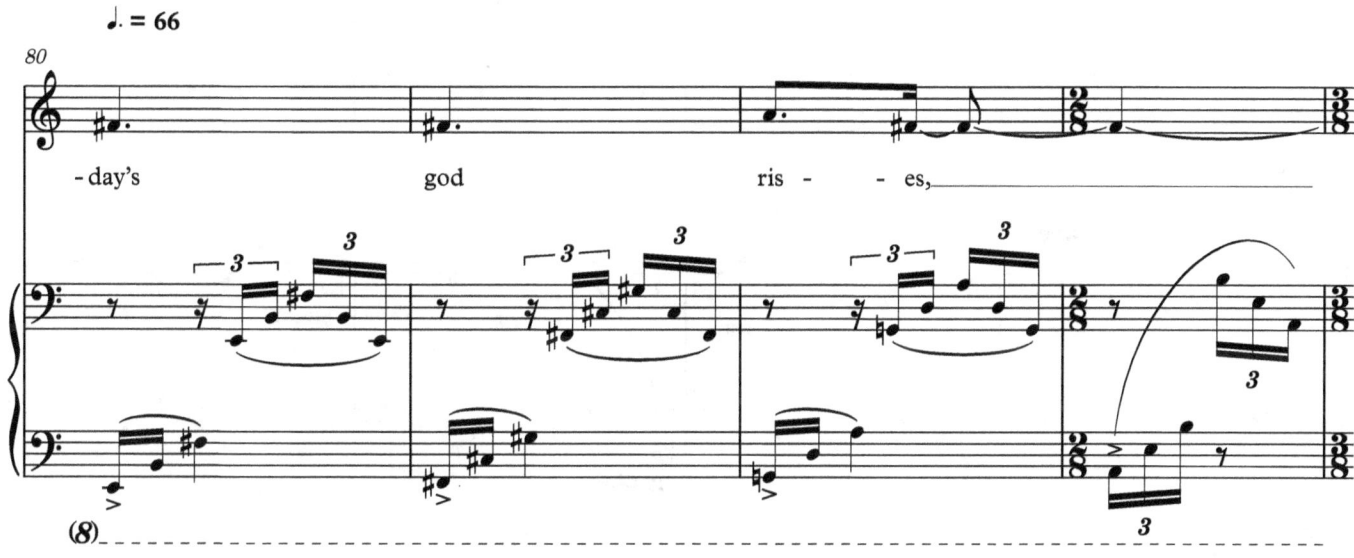
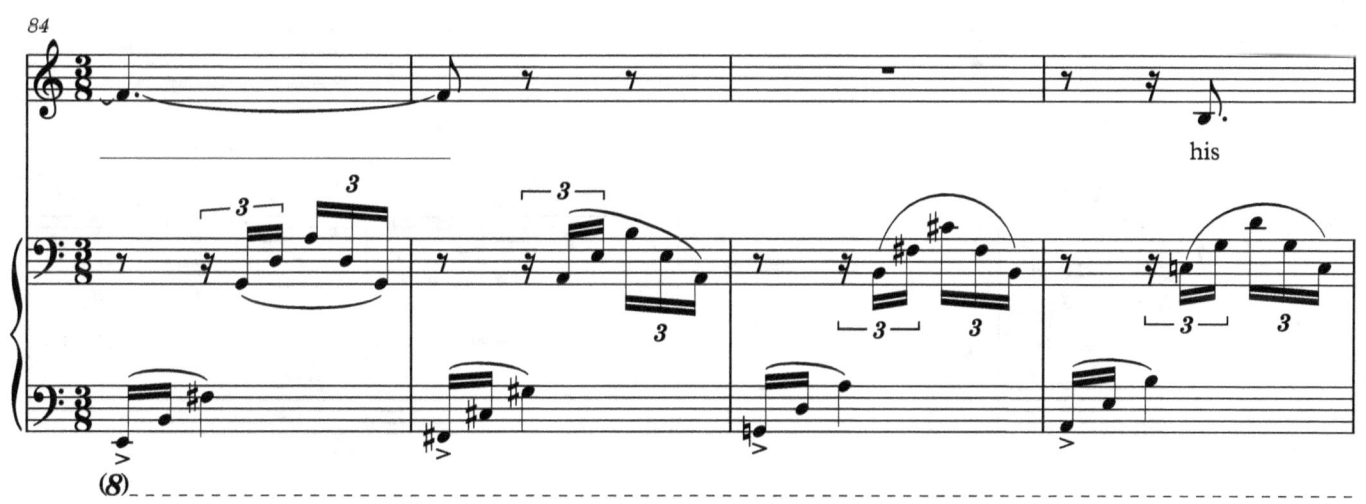

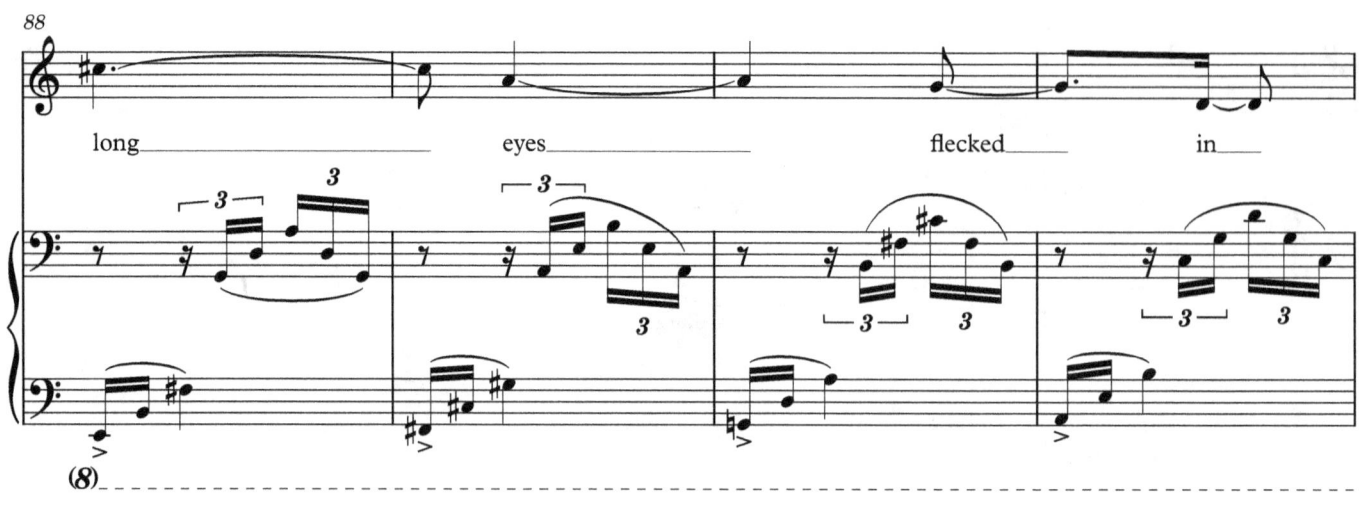
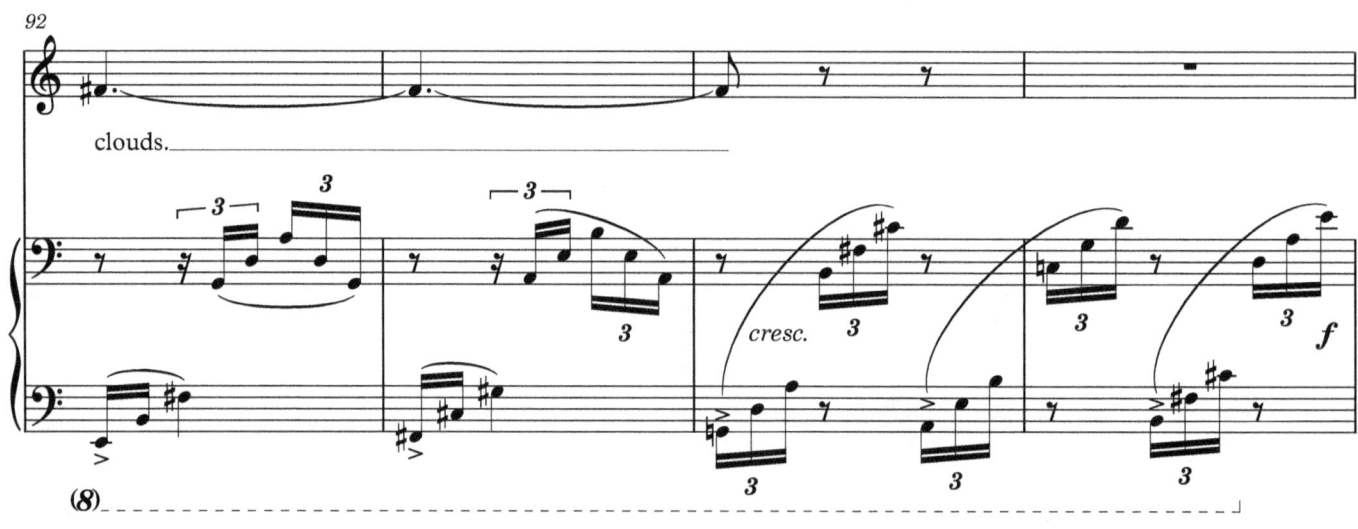

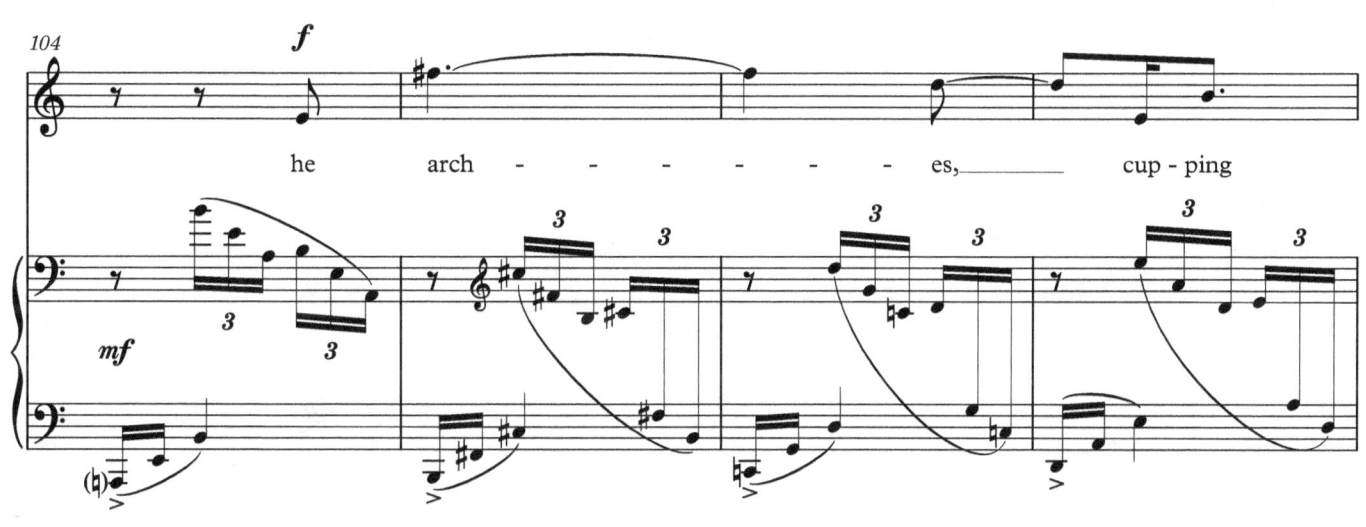

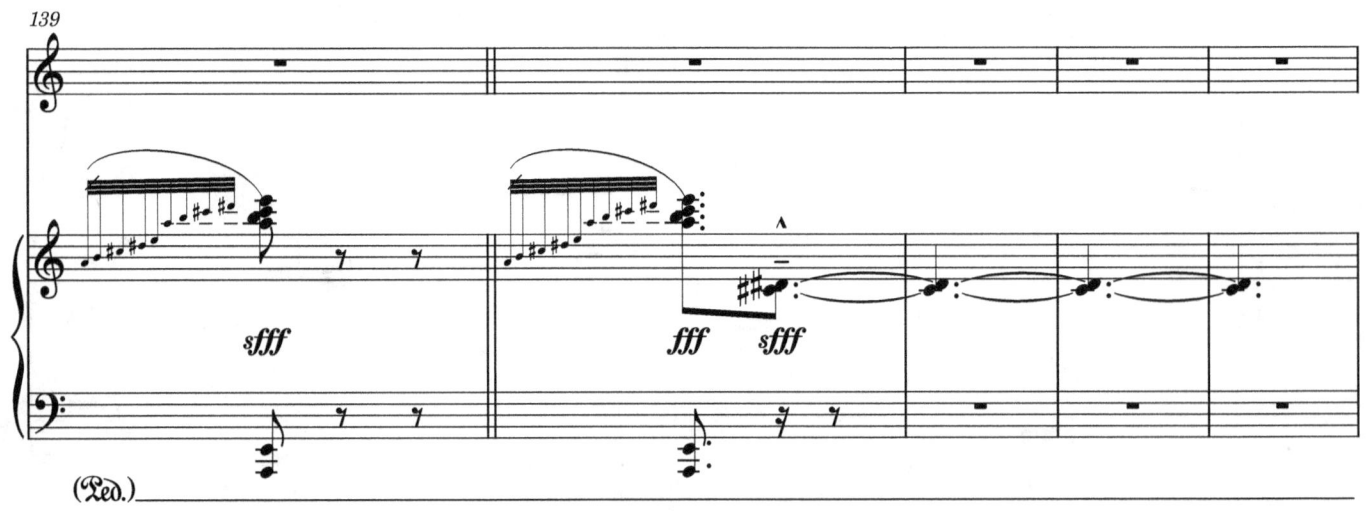
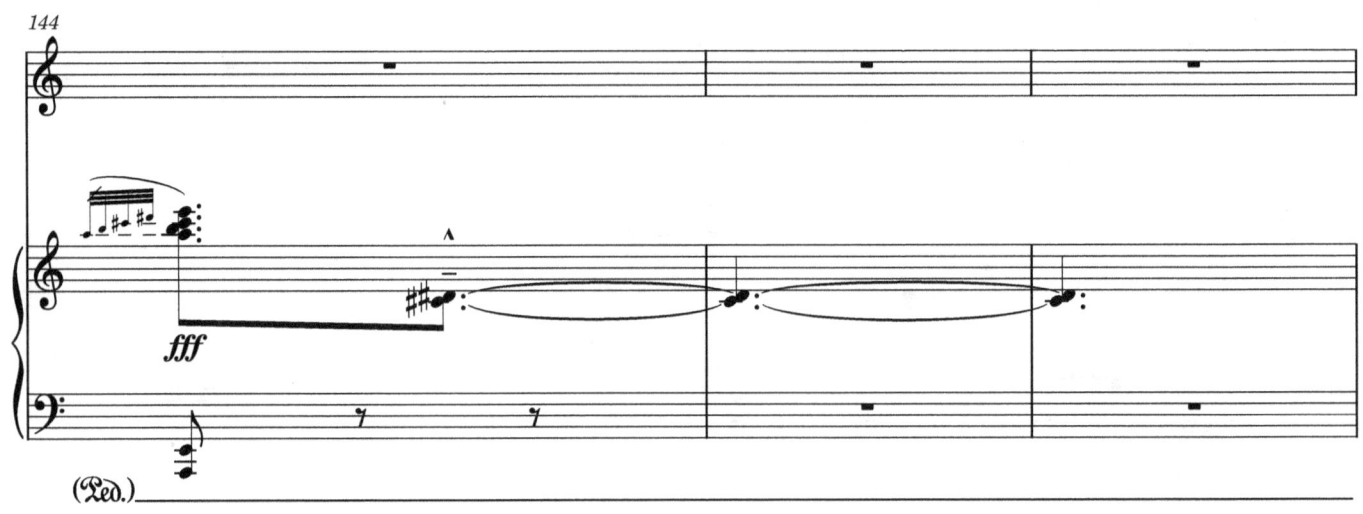
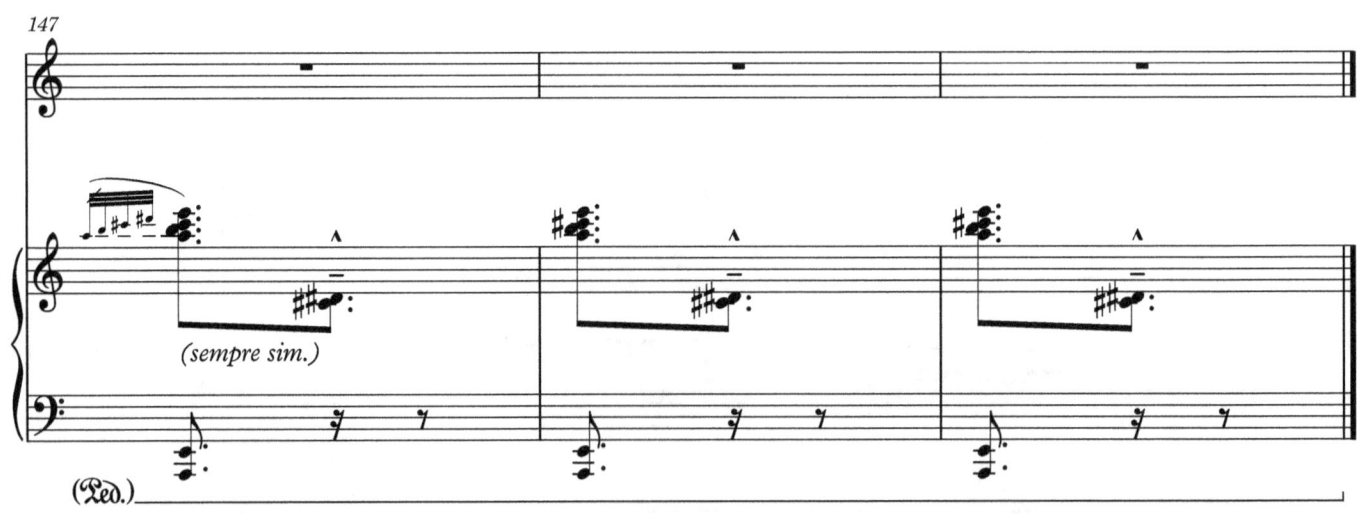

*for Renée Fleming*
# It Is Night
*from Three Persian Songs*

NIMA YUSHIJ  
BEHZAD RANJBARAN  
(1987)

**Adagio sostenuto** (♩. = 56)

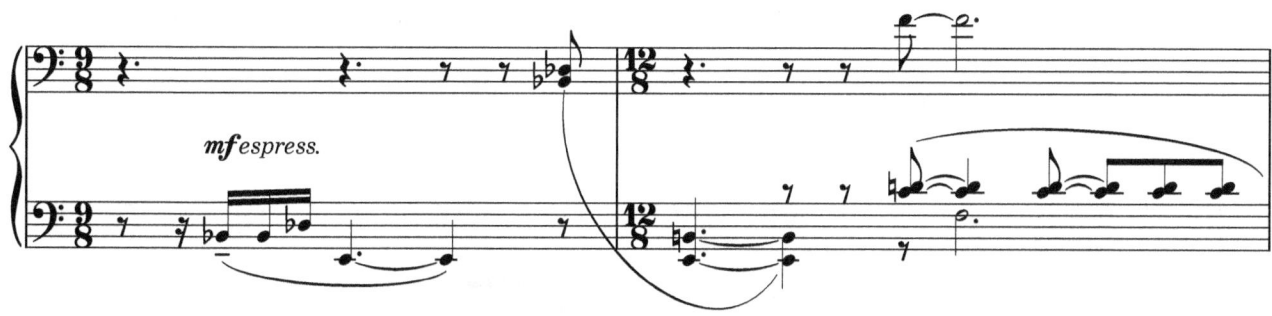

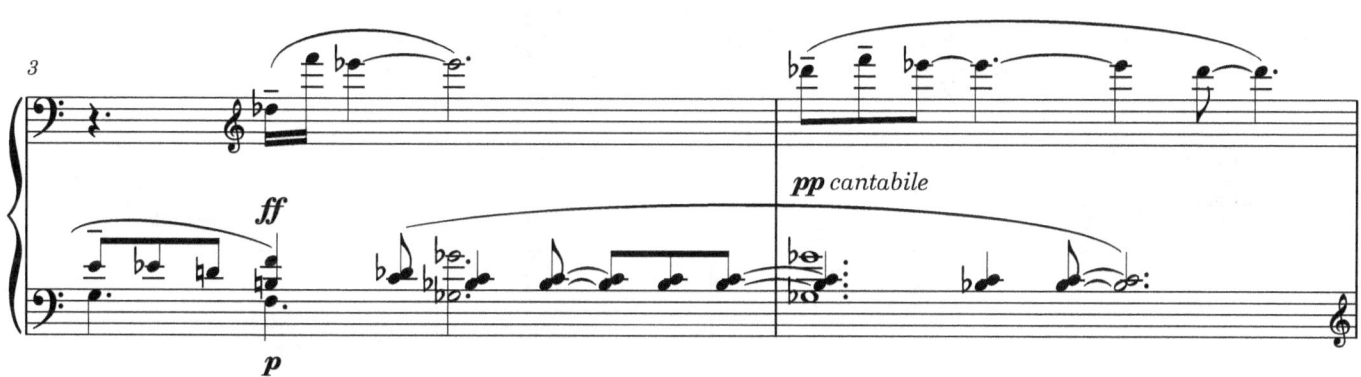

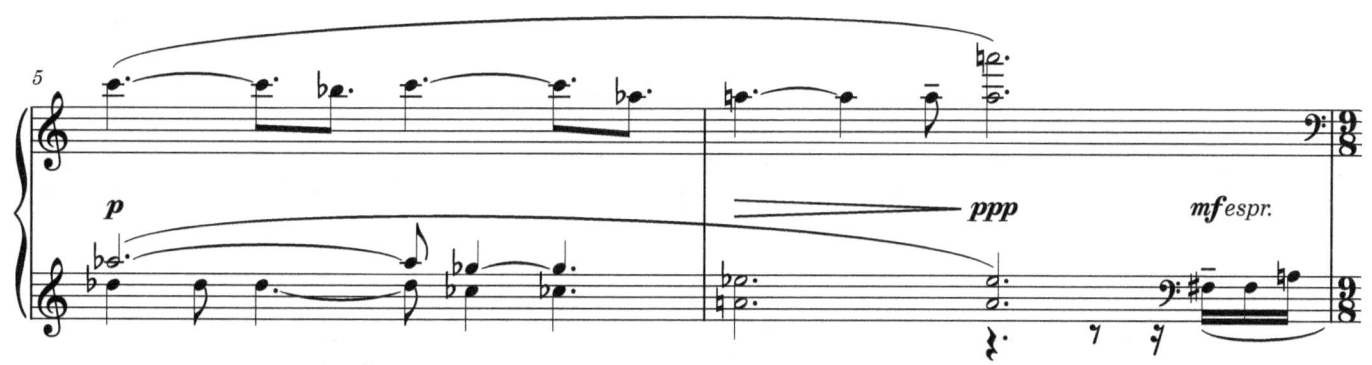

Copyright © 2013 by Theodore Presser Company. All Rights Reserved. International Copyright Secured.

144

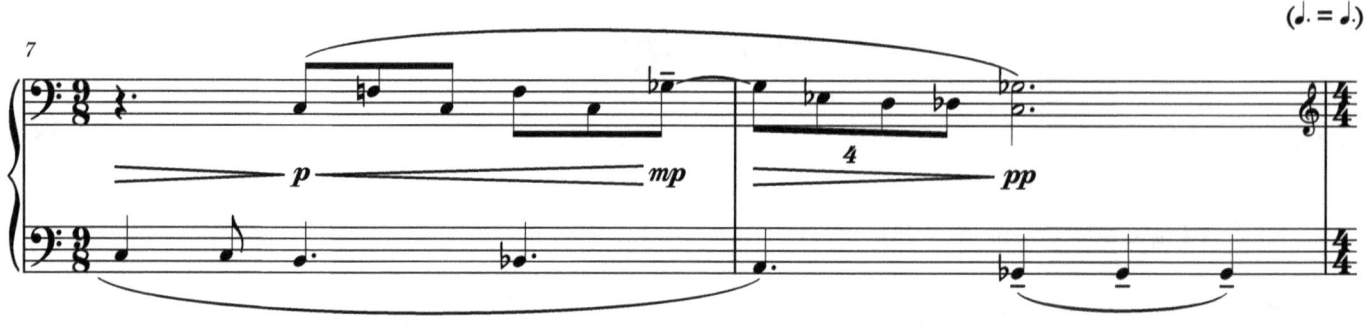

It is night, a damp night and the soil has

giv - en up its col - or.

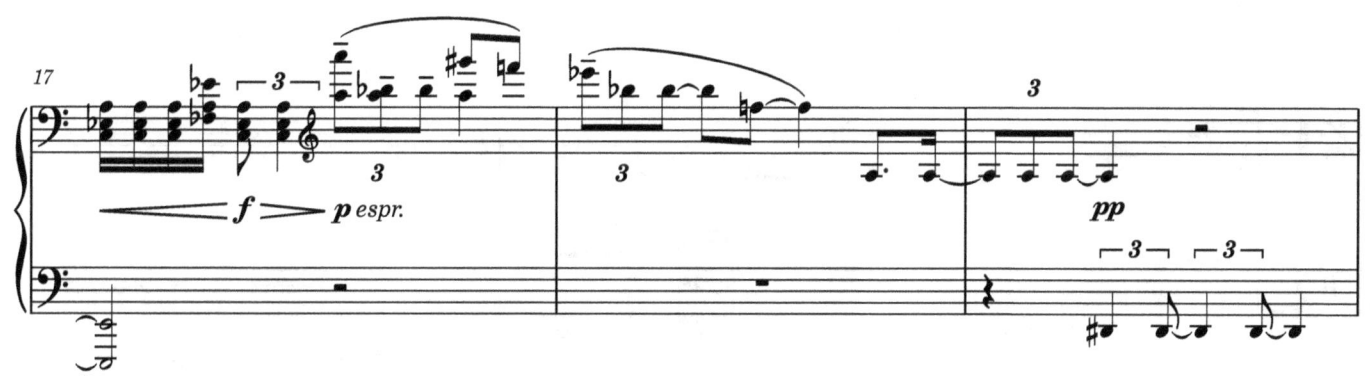

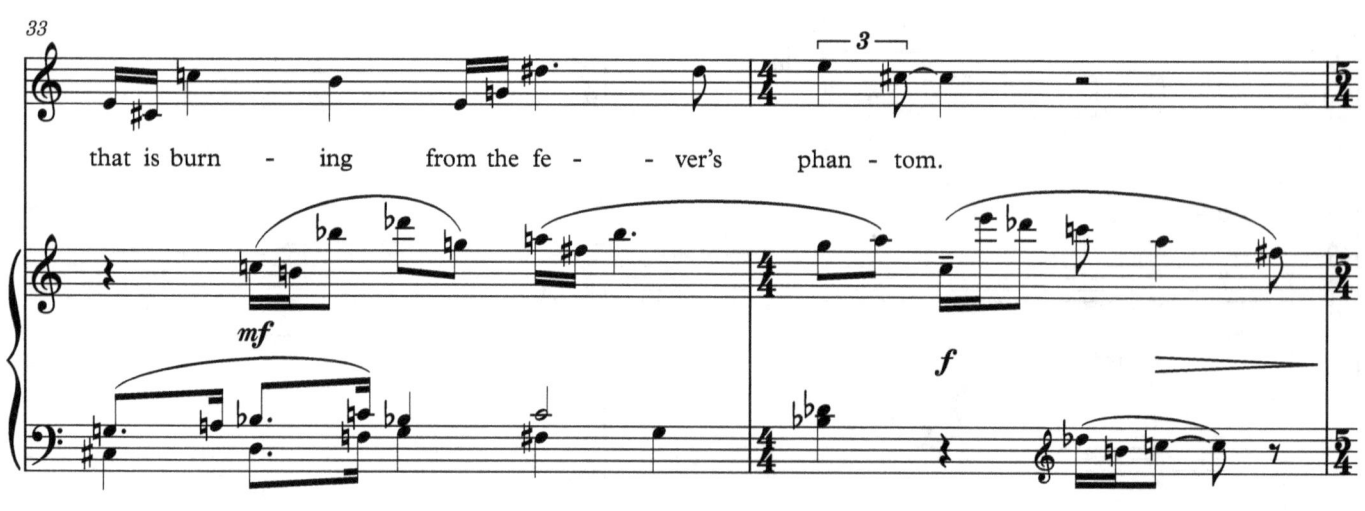

*for Nan Cui*
# Le Pont Mirabeau

GUILLAUME APOLLINAIRE　　　　　　　　　　　　　　　　　　　　　WILLIAM TOUTANT
(2015)

Sous le pont Mi-ra-beau cou-le la Sei-ne Et nos a-mours

Faut-il qu'il m'en sou-vien-ne La

Copyright © 2015 by William Toutant. All Rights Reserved.

150

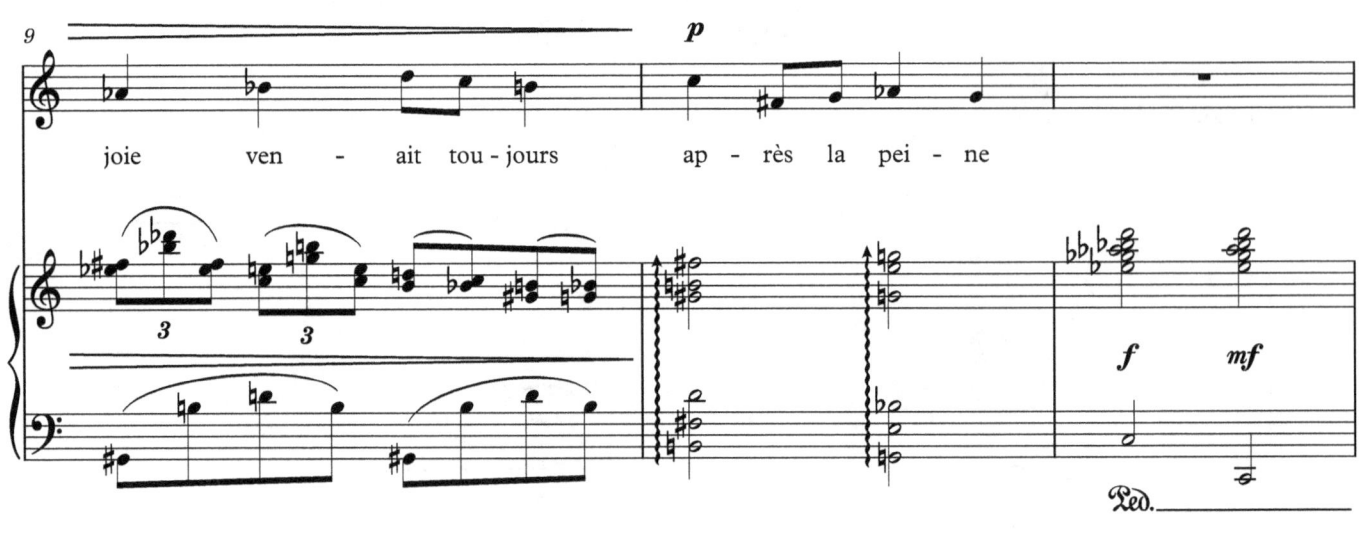

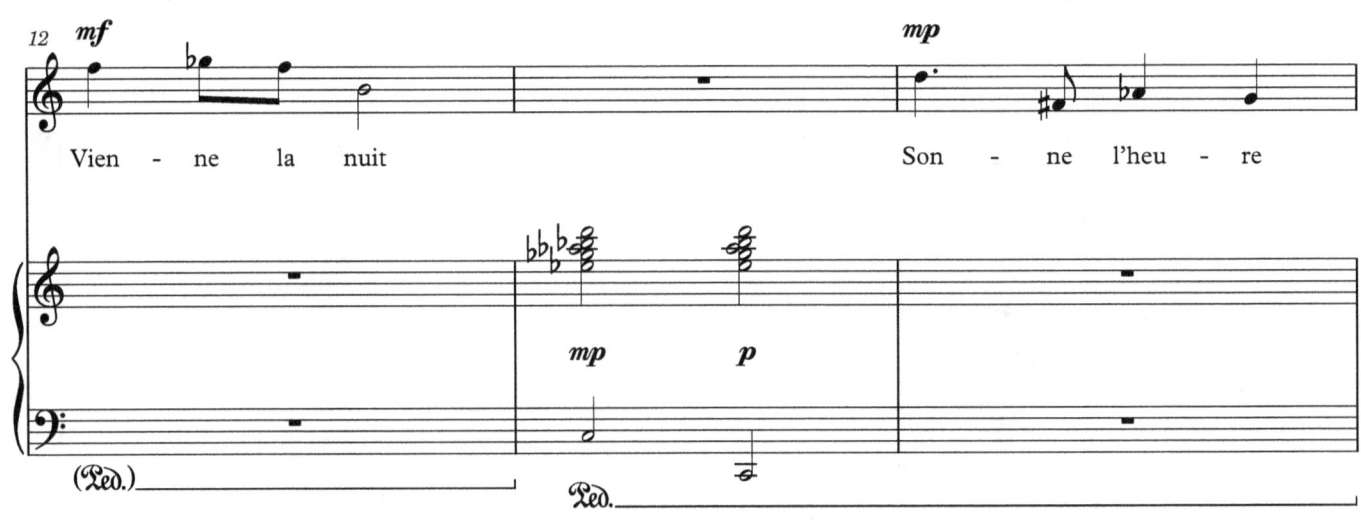

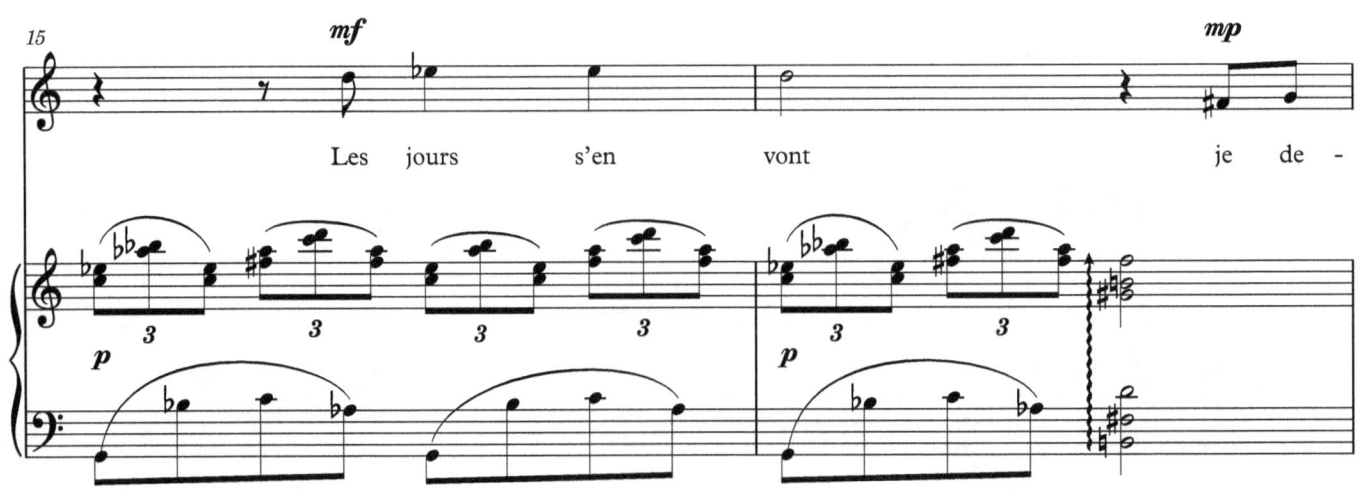

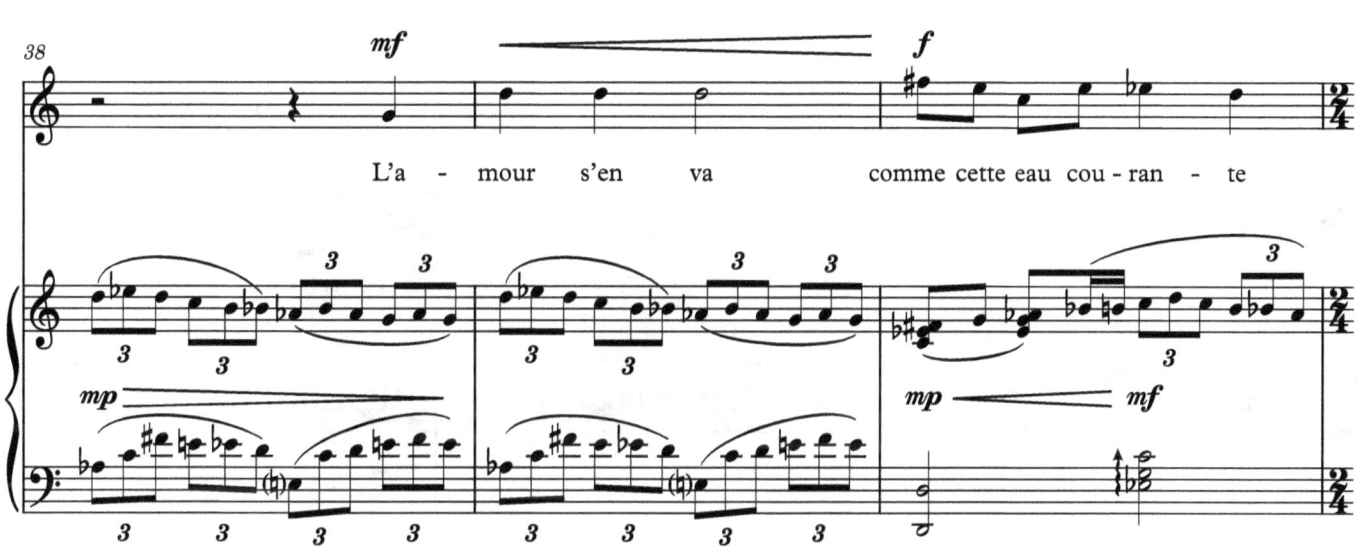

L'a - mour s'en va comme cette eau cou - ran - te

L'a - - mour s'en va  Comme la vie est len - te

156

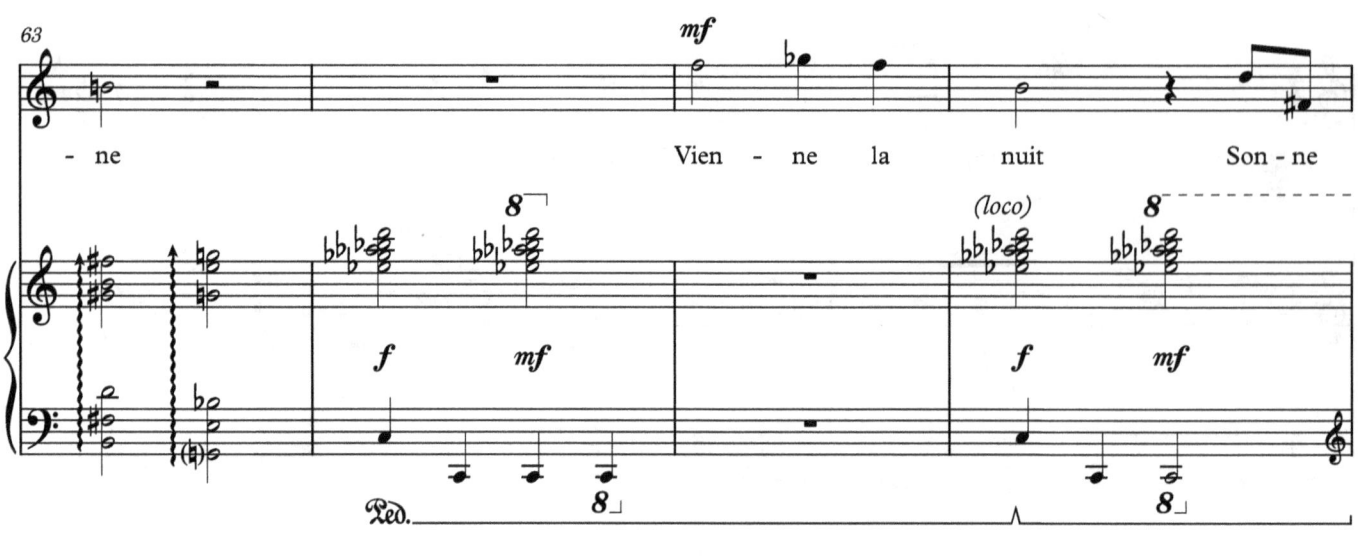

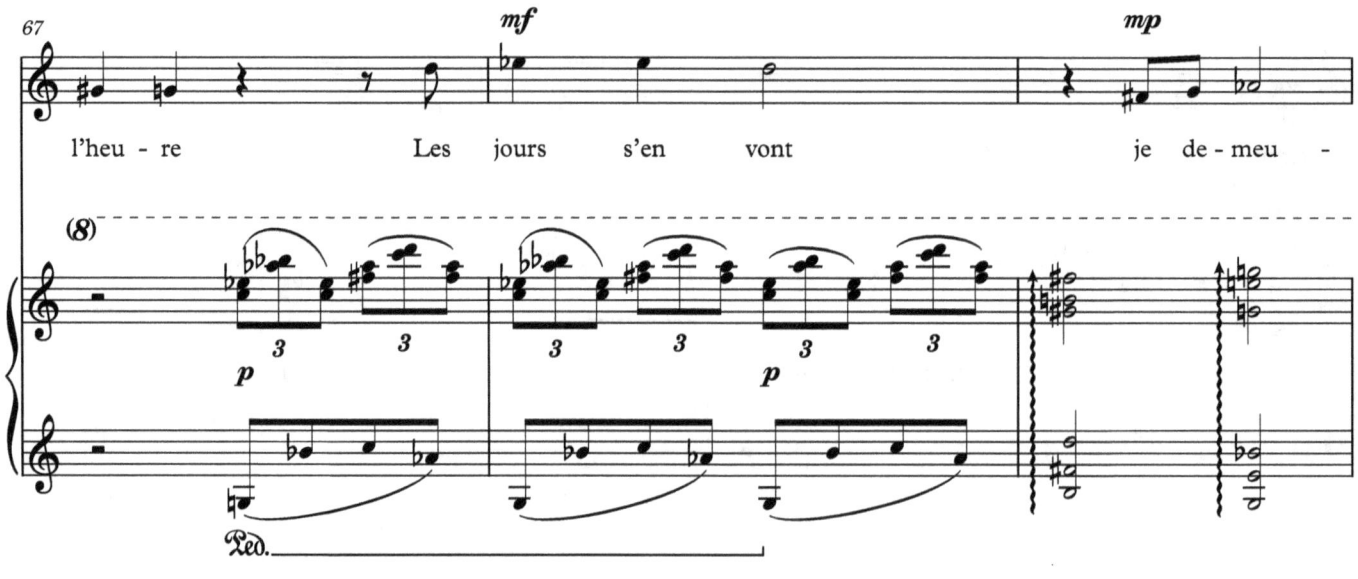

# Elegy Before Death
*from For Allegra*

EDNA ST. VINCENT MILLAY

THEODORE WIPRUD
(2010)

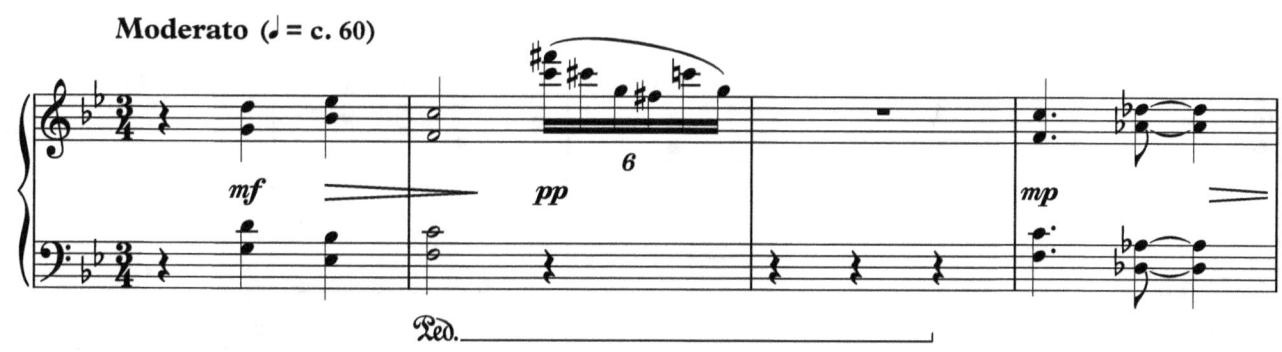

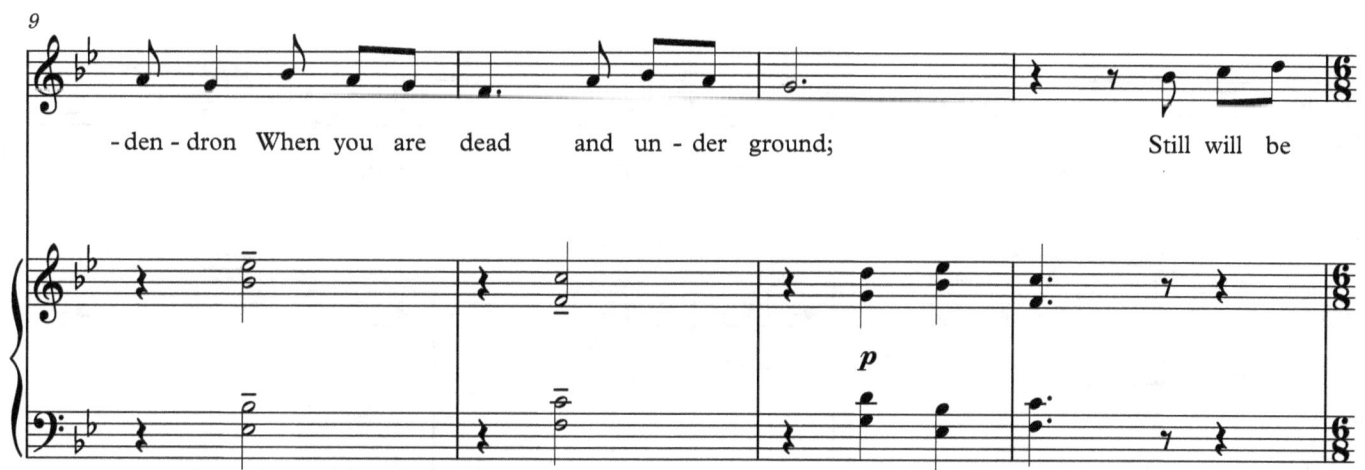

Copyright © 2010 Theodore Wiprud. All Rights Reserved.

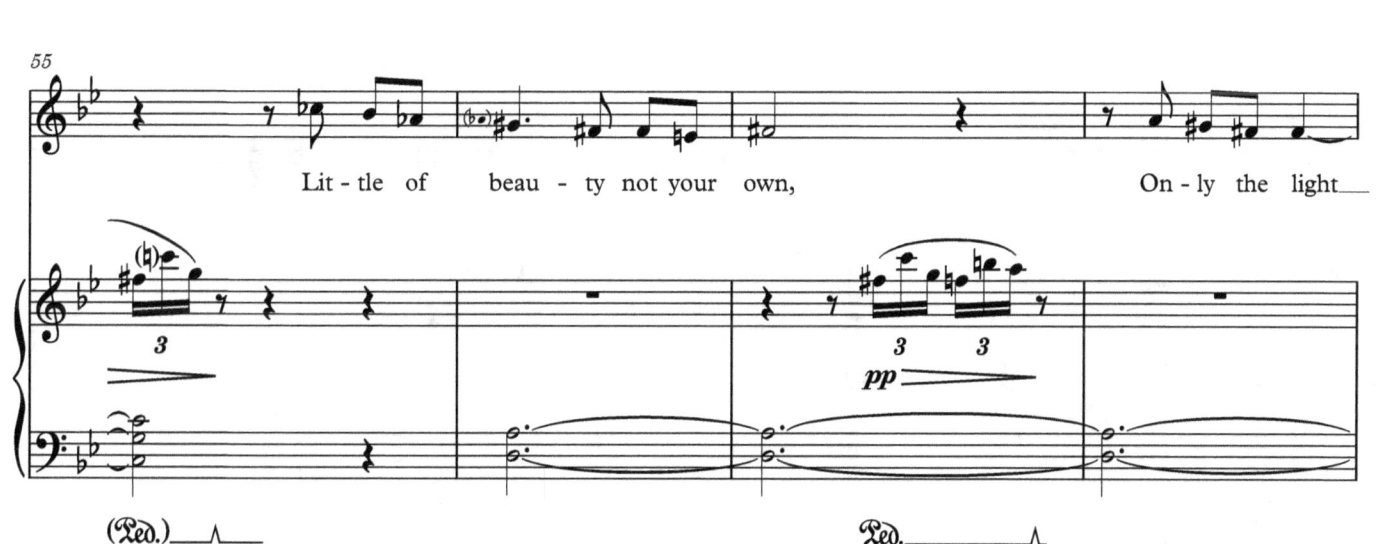

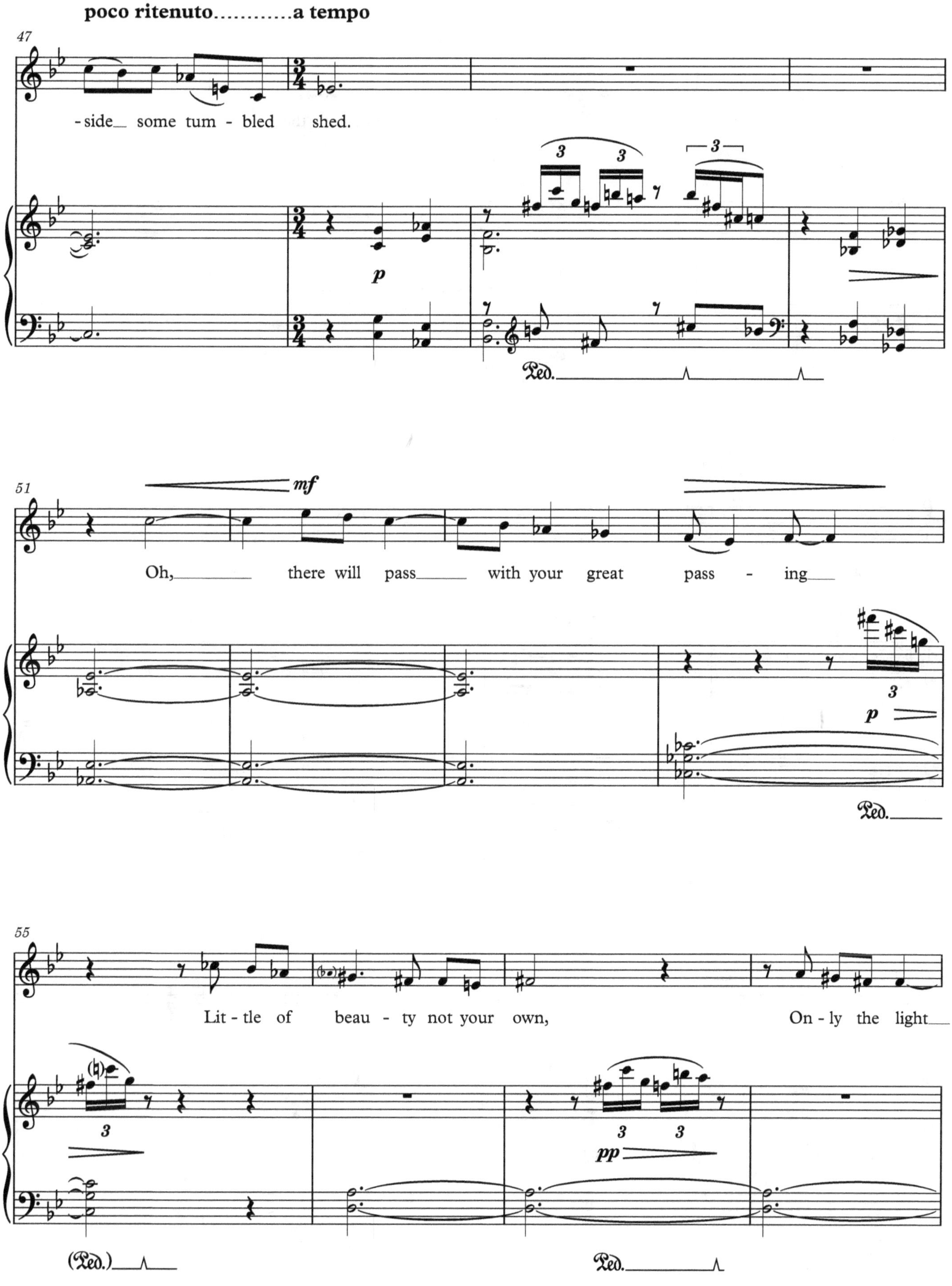
poco ritenuto............a tempo
47
-side__ some tum - bled shed.
p
Ped.
51
mf
Oh,______ there will pass______ with your great pass - ing__
p
Ped.
55
Lit - tle of beau - ty not your own, On - ly the light__
pp
(Ped.)
Ped.

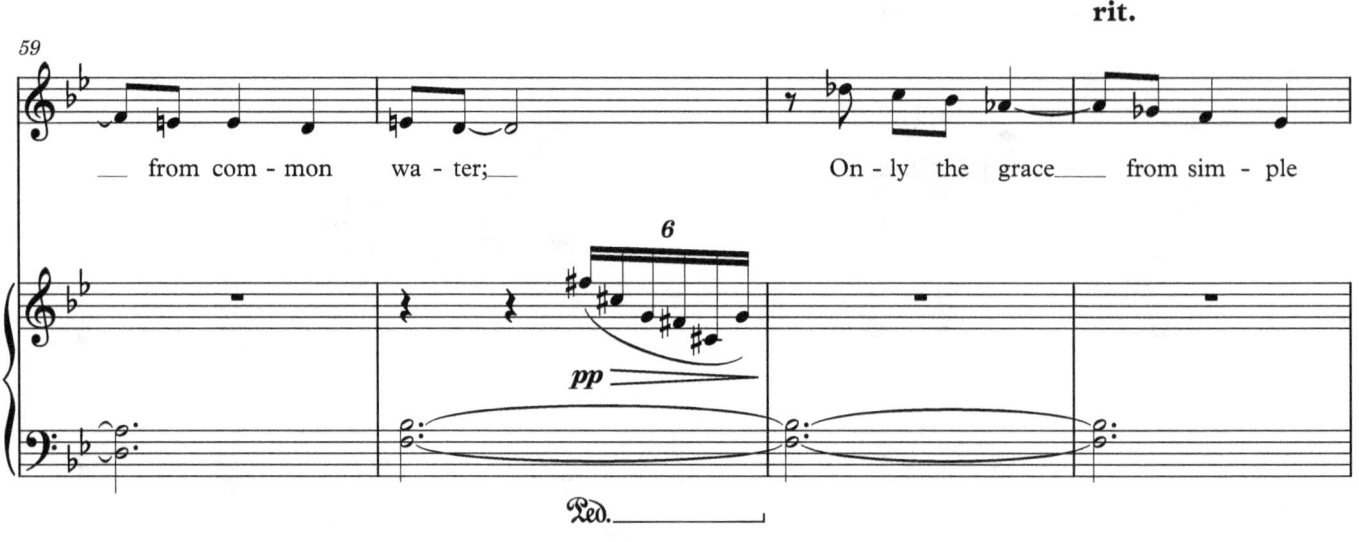
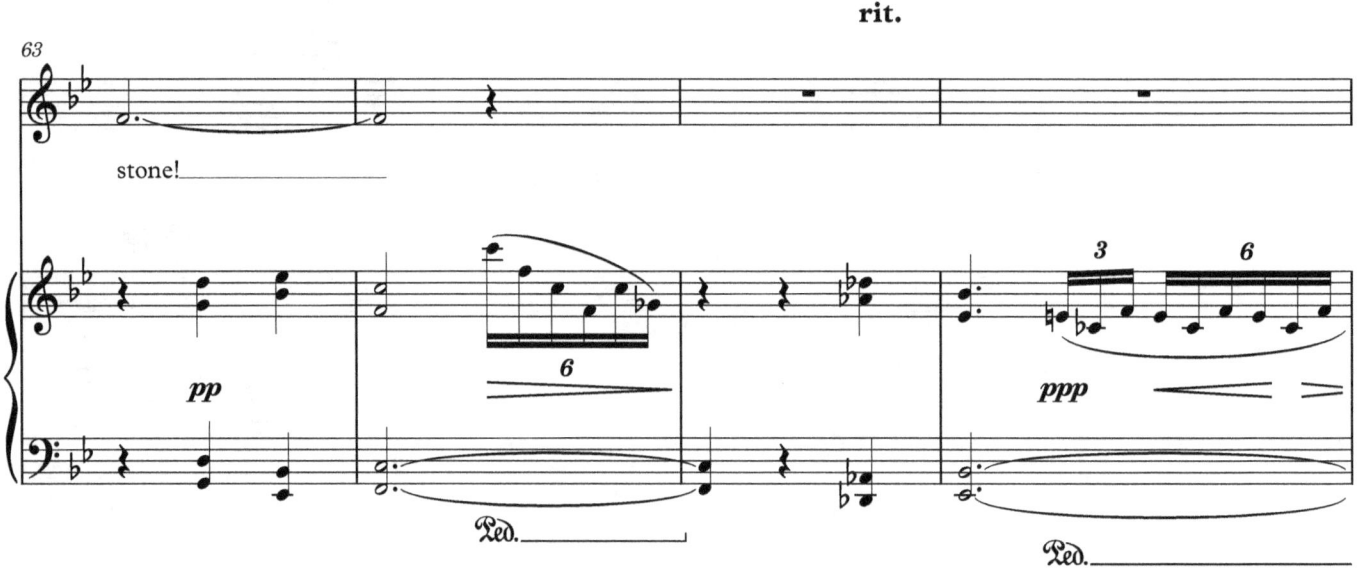
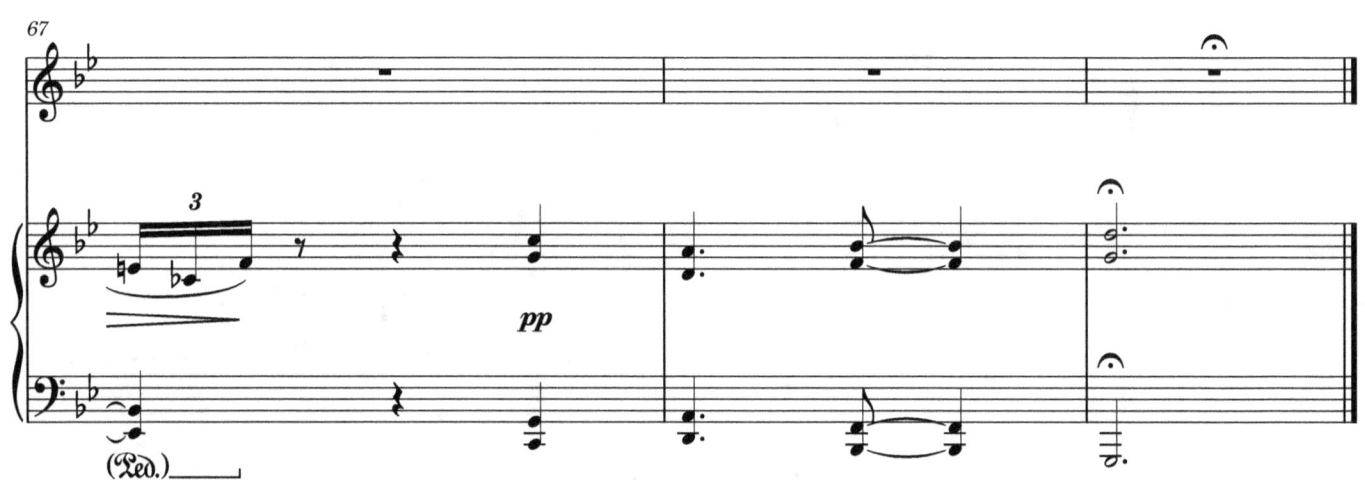

# About the Curator
# Laura Strickling

www.laurastrickling.com

Laura Strickling has been praised by *The New York Times* for her, "flexible voice, crystalline diction, and warm presence."

Ms. Strickling is an alumna of the Berkshire Opera Company resident artist program, where *Opera News* said of her performance of the Dew Fairy in Humperdinck's *Hansel and Gretel*, "Laura Strickling offered the creamy, clear, younger-sister-of-Eva-Pogner instrument ideal for singing the role over full orchestration." She appeared as Pamina in the Metropolitan Opera Guild's touring outreach production of *The Magic Flute*.

Her recording of James Matheson's *Times Alone* with Yarlung Records was hailed by *MusicWeb International* for, "shapely, nuanced voicings and emotional urgency...a striking directness." *New Voices*, the Billboard Classical Top-Ten-selling album including her recording of Glen Roven's *The Vineyard Songs* was acclaimed by *Opera News*, "Laura Strickling's lovely diction and warm, clear sound bring attractive immediacy to this cycle." She can also be heard on *New American Song @ SongFest*, performing Jake Heggie's *Edna St. Vincent Millay*, and on *The Garden: Songs and Vocal Chamber Works* by Tom Cipullo. *Confessions*, her first solo CD project of American art song, with pianist Joy Schreier, will be released in 2020.

Ms. Strickling was a vocal fellow at the Tanglewood Music Center in 2013 and 2014, a resident artist at the Steans Music Institute at Ravinia in 2012, a recipient of the Marc and Eva Stern Fellowship at SongFest in 2011 and 2012, and performed in The Song Continues…with Marilyn Horne – Weill Music Institute's 2012 Professional Training Program at Carnegie Hall. She received her Master of Music in Voice from the Peabody Institute of Johns Hopkins University and her Bachelor of Music in Sacred Music from the Moody Bible Institute.

A Chicago native, Ms. Strickling is an avid traveler, having lived in Fez, Morocco, where she studied classical Arabic, and Kabul, Afghanistan, where her husband was the founding chair of the Department of Law at the American University of Afghanistan. She currently makes her home in St. Thomas, U. S. Virgin Islands. For further information, visit www.laurastrickling.com.

# About the Composers

# John Arrigo-Nelson

**b. 1975**

arrigomusic@gmail.com
www.arrigomusic.com

John Arrigo-Nelson's music has been performed and broadcast throughout the United States and in Europe. Recent seasons have seen the premieres of solo and chamber works in New York City, Houston, Baltimore, Minneapolis, and Cincinnati. His awards and recognition include a MacDowell Colony Residency, Wellesley Composers Conference Fellowship, and Stony Brook University's Ackerman Prize. His music addresses ideas of timbral and temporal flexibility, and explores how contextual variation and fragmentation affect perception and function. John has studied at the Internationales Musikinstitut Darmstadt with Olga Neuwirth, Isabel Mundry and Salvatore Sciarrino and holds a Ph.D. from Stony Brook University, where his primary teachers were Daria Semegen and Sheila Silver. He is an Artistic Team member of the contemporary music collective Alia Musica Pittsburgh, and also serves as the ensemble's guitarist. John has been an adjunct faculty member at the University of Notre Dame, Indiana University South Bend, Suffolk County Community College, and Stony Brook University, teaching theory, musicianship, and composition.

# Paul Ayres

b. 1970

paulayres@clara.net
www.paulayres.co.uk

Paul Ayres was born in London (UK), studied music at Oxford University, and now works freelance as a composer & arranger, choral conductor & musical director, and organist & accompanist. He has received over one hundred commissions, and his works have been awarded or shortlisted for composition prizes in Bulgaria, Canada, Croatia, New Zealand, Poland, Russia, Spain, Switzerland, the UK and the USA. Paul particularly enjoys "re-composing" classical works (Purcell, Bach, Handel, Fauré) and "classicizing" pop music (jazz and show tunes, The Beatles, Happy Hardcore).

Most of Paul's compositions involve words, in pieces for solo voice, for choir, and for theatre. He collaborates with several poets, lyricists and librettists, and has set existing texts in Aramaic, ancient Greek, and West Yorkshire dialect. Stage works include the children's opera *The Stolen Moon*, the family opera *Just So: Tegumai's Tales*, and the two-hander *For Sale* (whose entire libretto is "For Sale. Baby Shoes. Never Worn.")

Of his solo CD *Handel-Inspired* (Priory), *The Gramophone* wrote: "Ayres is outstanding as composer, arranger, editor and skilful player... this CD is undoubtedly one of the most enjoyable and original recordings I've heard."

Paul is the regular conductor of City Chorus and the London College of Music Chorus (at the University of West London), accompanist of Concordia Voices, and associate accompanist of Crouch End Festival Chorus. He has led many music education workshops for children, and played piano for improvised comedy shows and musical theatre. Please visit www.paulayres.co.uk to find out more.

# Clint Borzoni (ASCAP)

b. 1981

clintborzoni@gmail.com
www.clintborzoni.com

Clint Borzoni is an award-winning composer whose "highly original yet lyrical music...[and] natural gift for melody and harmonic structure" (*The Huffington Post*) has resulted in international performances and premieres.

His first opera with John de los Santos, *When Adonis Calls*, was premiered by Ashville Lyric Opera in May 2018, and will receive a second production by Thompson Street Opera and the Chicago Pride Center in September 2018. The full-length piece has also been presented by Fort Worth Opera, the Merola Opera Program, Opera America's New Works Forum, and operamission. Their second opera, *The Copper Queen*, won the top prize for Arizona Opera's commission program, Arizona SPARK, and is currently being developed by Arizona Opera. Borzoni's other operatic works have been performed by La MaMA, Symphony Space, the Glimmerglass Festival, the American Lyric Theater, the American Opera Projects, Opera on Tap, the Morgan Library & Museum, St Martin-in-the-Fields, and the Guildhall School of Music.

Mr. Borzoni has composed songs and song cycles for many leading vocalists. He won BARIHUNKS Best New Song (2015) and Best New Solo Work for Baritone (2017). He was also a winner of Sparks & Wiry Cries Second annual NYC songSLAM, and operamission's cabaret song competition.

Mr. Borzoni is the current Composer-in-Residence for Musica Marin, a nonprofit organization that presents, supports and inspires classical music throughout the San Francisco Bay Area. He studied with Pulitzer Prize-winning composer David Del Tredici at the City University of New York where he received an MA in Music Composition. He lives and works as a composer and teacher in NYC.

**Facebook:** www.facebook.com/clintborzonicomposer/
**Twitter:** @clintborzoni

# Mark Buller

b. 1986

www.markbullercomposer.com

The music of composer and pianist Mark Buller has been performed around the country and internationally, in a variety of venues: Carnegie Hall, the Wortham Center (Houston), and Movimento (Munich), as well as further locations in Europe, South America, and Asia.

Current commissions and projects include a concerto for English horn, a fourth string quartet, two operas, art songs, and orchestrations for ROCO (River Oaks Chamber Orchestra).

Buller has composed three operas to date, all in collaboration with librettist and poet Charles Anthony Silvestri. The first, *The Pastry Prince*, was premiered by Houston Grand Opera in January 2015. The success of this opera led to the commission of a follow-up, *The Puffed-Up Prima Donna*. These two operas have been performed a combined total of 180 times to date. A third opera with Silvestri, *The Trial of Alice*, was commissioned by the Houston Girls Chorus. Buller was named the national winner of the Rapido! Composition Contest, for *Regressive Variations*. His works have also won the Vanguard Voices Choral Composition Competition (for *Sicut Cervus*, which was subsequently performed at Carnegie Hall) and the Sarofim Composition Award. Recent performances include the war oratorio *Of Shrapnel and Blood* by the Greenbriar Consortium; a flute concerto by flutist Aaron Perdue at Rice University; *Motion Studies* by Boston Musica Viva, Voices of Change (Dallas), Atlanta Chamber Players, and Detroit Chamber Winds & Strings; *The Songs of Ophelia* by the Atlanta Symphony Orchestra and director Robert Spano; orchestrated versions of *Nursery Rhymes* and *Tombstone Songs* featuring baritone Timothy Jones with River Oaks Chamber Orchestra; and *Overboard*, a 10-minute choral work commissioned by Houston Grand Opera.

Buller earned his DMA at the University of Houston, where he studied with Marcus Maroney and Rob Smith. He currently teaches composition and ear training at Lone Star College, is the program annotator for ROCO, works in audience engagement for Musiqa, and is the Education and Outreach Manager for AFA, Houston's largest nonprofit provider of music education.

# Martin Bussey

b. 1958

www.martinbussey.co.uk

Martin Bussey is a noted musician and educationist, combining the roles of composer, singer and conductor with his work for the Independent Schools Inspectorate. He was born in London in 1958 and educated at Haberdasher's Aske's School, Elstree before reading music as a choral scholar at King's College, Cambridge. He studied singing with John Carol Case and composition with Robin Holloway. He undertook postgraduate study at the Royal Northern College of Music.

Martin taught at Chetham's School of Music from 1988 to 2013, including as Head of Music in the Curriculum and Director of Choirs, performing on disc and at the BBC Proms. Martin sings with and directs The BBC Daily Service Singers, and is a vocal tutor at The University of Manchester.

Martin is an experienced and versatile composer with a varied catalogue of works. His interests include song, choral music for a variety of forces, and organ music, as well as instrumental works. His larger scale choral works have been well received, beginning with *The Pied Piper* (1985) and *A Brand Plucked from the Burning* (1989), his cantata celebrating the life and work of John Wesley. There have been many performances of his song cycles setting individual poets: *A Chainless Soul* (Emily Bronte), *Poems of 1912/13* (Thomas Hardy) and *Blue Remembered Hills* (A E Housman). His choral music includes challenging a capella works, such as *Ave Maria* and *Christ is the Morning Star*, as well as simpler, accompanied music, for example, *Listen Sweet Dove* (Whitsunday). Many audiences have enjoyed his choral arrangements of classics such as *I've Got You Under My Skin*, *The Carnival is Over*, and *Sentimental Journey*.

He has a great interest in the connection between words and music, giving regular recital and lecture programmes focussing on settings of individual poets (Housman, Hardy and Gurney) and the output of English song composers in general. In this capacity he is chairman of the Finzi Friends committee where he is active in promoting workshops for young performers and composers.

# Emerson Eads (ASCAP)

b. 1980

emersoneads@gmail.com
www.emersoneads.com

Composer and conductor, Dr. Emerson Eads has devoted himself to music of social concern.

His *Mass for the Oppressed*, a setting of the Ordinary of the Mass featuring textual interpolations by his brother Evan Eads, and a Credo adapted from the diary of Pope Francis before his ordination, holds particular poignancy for the social issues of our time. The *Mass* was written for the release of the Fairbanks Four (native Alaskan's from the composer's home town) who spent 18 years in prison wrongfully. His newest cantata "…from which your laughter rises." for mezzo-soprano, oboe, and orchestra, was written for the mothers of the Fairbanks Four, and was paired in a concert featuring Haydn's *Stabat Mater*, conducted to acclaim. His newest opera, *The Princess Sophia*, about the sinking of the SS Princess Sophia in October of 1918, will be premiered in Juneau, Alaska in October 25th, 2018.

Dr. Eads studied choral conducting with Carmen-Helena Tellez at the University of Notre Dame working with eminent choral conductors such as, Joseph Flummerfelt, Stephen Cleobury, Anne Howard Jones, and Peter Phillips among others. He studied composition with Alaskan composer John Luther Adams. He currently is Director of Choral Activities at Minot State University.

# Evan Fein

**b. 1984**

www.evanfein.com

American composer Evan Fein was born in Cleveland, Ohio and currently resides in New York City, where he serves on the faculty of The Juilliard School Pre-College and Evening Divisions. His music, known for its strongly lyrical and narrative qualities, has been widely performed at home and abroad — including in France, Germany, China, Iceland, the United Kingdom, and the Netherlands. He was awarded the Palmer Dixon Prize for Outstanding Composition, is the recipient of honors from the ASCAP Foundation, Boston Metro Opera, and the American Scandinavian Society, and additionally serves as Chair of the Music Committee for the Board of Trustees of the Oratorio Society of New York.

Evan Fein has served as Composer-in-Residence (Artiste Associé) for the Paris-based chamber opera troupe Opéra de Poche since 2012. His first opera, *The Raven's Kiss*, based on Icelandic folk stories, was premiered in concert at Juilliard in 2011. His second, *L'Île des sept sœurs*, a Southern Gothic tale, was given its premiere in Paris in 2013 by Opéra de Poche. *City of Ashes*, which follows the stories of two German women in the days immediately following the fall of Berlin in 1945, was presented by Opéra de Poche in 2015 in Paris and again in Beijing in 2016. His major work for chorus and orchestra, *Deborah*, an oratorio based on the Book of Judges, was premiered by Musica Sacra at Alice Tully Hall at Lincoln Center in 2016.

Evan Fein holds a Doctorate of Musical Arts and a Master of Music from The Juilliard School and a Bachelor of Music from the Cleveland Institute of Music. In addition, he pursued auxiliary studies at the Freie Universität Berlin (FUBiS) and L'École Normale de Musique de Paris (EAMA). His primary teachers included Robert Beaser, Samuel Adler, Michel Merlet, and Margaret Brouwer.

His dissertation *"The Ghosts of Versailles" by John Corigliano: An Evolutionary Study* was completed in 2014. The first comprehensive study of the work commissioned by the Metropolitan Opera for its centennial, it is now available to scholars around the world. Equally at home in cinema, Evan holds an IMDb credit as primary orchestrator on the 2011 film Sedona, featuring Frances Fisher.

# Daniel Felsenfeld

b. 1970

www.daniel-felsenfeld.com

Composer Daniel Felsenfeld has been commissioned and performed by Simone Dinnerstein, Opera On Tap, UrbanArias, Metropolis Ensemble, The Crossing/ICE, Meerenai Shim, the New York Philharmonic New Music Biennial, NANOWorks Opera, Kathleen Supovè, ASCAP, San Jose Opera, ETHEL, Great Noise Ensemble, American Opera Projects, the Da Capo Chamber Players, Cadillac Moon Ensemble, Nadia Sirota, and New York City Opera (VOX), and as part of the BEAT Festival, MATA Festival, Make Music New York, Ecstatic Music Festival, Opera Grows in Brooklyn, and John Wesley Harding's Cabinet of Wonders. When rapper Jay-Z performed in Carnegie Hall, along with Alicia Keys and Nas, backed by a full orchestra, Felsenfeld was asked to do all of the orchestrations and arrangements. He also collaborated with The Roots (offering music on their Grammy-nominated record Undun, appearing with them and the Metropolis Ensemble on the Jimmy Fallon Show) and ?uestlove with Keren Ann and David Murray. He also wrote arrangements for noth ShuffleCulture and Electronium, shows at the Brooklyn Academy of Music with ?uestlove, Sasha Grey, Deerhoof, Reggie Watts, and How to Dress Well and the Metropolis Ensemble. He is also the Court Composer for John Wesley Harding's Cabinet of Wonders, for which he wrote the theme—and which can be heard as an NPR Podcast. Residencies include Yaddo, the MacDowell Colony, The Hermitage, and the Atlantic Center for the Arts.

Felsenfeld is also an accomplished essayist, annotator, and author, with eight books to his name as well as articles for the New York Times, Listen, Playbill, Time Out New York, Symphony Magazine, Strings Magazine, NewMusicBox, and Early Music Magazine; program notes for the Metropolitan Opera, New York City Opera, Philadelphia Orchestra, Miller Theatre, Wigmore Hall, and Carnegie Hall; liner notes for Naxos, Bridge, Koch, EMI, Sony, and Adjustable Music. He served as curator for The Score in the Opinionator Section of the New York Times, he co-founded the New Music Gathering (an annual conference-concert series hybrid) which took place in San Francisco in 2015, as well as for Music After, a marathon concert on 9.11.11 he co-produced with Eleonor Sandresky. He is a teaching artist at the New York Philharmonic's Very Young Composers program, and lives in Brooklyn with his wife and daughter.

# Jodi Goble (ASCAP)

**b. 1974**

goblejs@gmail.com
www.jodigoble.com

Composer Jodi Goble writes text-based, character-driven music fueled by her extensive background as a vocal coach and song-specialist collaborative pianist. Her compositions are praised for their melodism, their intuitive, idiomatic vocal writing, and the clarity and deftness of their text settings, and have been performed across the United States and internationally and featured on National Public Radio. She is the 2013 winner of the Iowa Music Teachers Association Commission Competition and the 2017 runner-up in the National Association of Teachers of Singing Art Song Competition. She also placed as a NATS ASCA finalist in 2008 and as the honorable mention winner in 2016.

Ms. Goble's works have recently been performed at the ASEAN Festival of Contemporary Music, Songfest, Beijing Central Conservatory, the Ames Town and Gown Musicale, Omaha Under the Radar, Boston University, the Massachusetts Institute of Technology, the University of Nebraska-Omaha, Scripps College, Curry College, Hunan Women's University, Endicott College, Iowa Composers' Forum, and the Art Song Preservation Society of New York. De Virginibus, her song cycle on texts by Hildegard von Bingen, was recorded by soprano Anne Harley as part of the Voices of the Pearl project.

Until 2009, Goble was a member of the voice faculty at Boston University's College of Fine Arts, senior vocal coach and Coordinator of Opera Programs for the Boston University Tanglewood Institute, and primary rehearsal pianist of the Boston Symphony Orchestra's Tanglewood Festival Chorus. Now Senior Lecturer in Voice at Iowa State University and recent recipient of the ISU Early Achievement in Teaching Award, Ms. Goble collaborates regularly in recital with bass-baritone Simon Estes and is the pianist and artistic director for the Simon Estes Young Artist Concert Series. She is the official pianist of the Metropolitan Opera Guild Auditions in Iowa and recitals regularly with artists affiliated with Des Moines Metro Opera.

Ms. Goble holds bachelor's degrees in violin and piano performance from Olivet Nazarene University and a M.M. in collaborative piano and chamber music from Ball State University.

# Juliana Hall (ASCAP)

b. 1958

JH@JulianaHall.com
www.julianahall.com

American art song composer Juliana Hall (b. 1958) is a prolific and highly-regarded composer of vocal music, whose songs have been described as "brilliant" (Washington Post), "beguiling" (Times of London), and "the most genuinely moving music of the afternoon" (Boston Globe). Hall has composed works for renowned countertenor Brian Asawa, acclaimed mezzo soprano Stephanie Blythe, and star soprano Dawn Upshaw, as well as for numerous organizations including Feminine Musique, Lynx Project, Lyric Fest, and the Seattle Art Song Society. Venues across America and worldwide including Carnegie Hall's Weill Recital Hall, the Library of Congress, Morgan Library & Museum, and Wigmore Hall, as well as the London Festival of American Music, Norfolk Chamber Music Festival, Ojai Music Festival, and Tanglewood Music Center have all hosted her work. St. Paul's Cathedral in London presented Hall's songs in a Holy Week meditation service in 2015, and the Joy in Singing organization in New York presented her songs on their "Edward T. Cone Composers Concert" at Lincoln Center in 2016. In 2017 Hall received SongFest's Sorel Commission, and in 2018 she was Guest Composer at the Fall Island Vocal Arts Seminar. Concerts devoted to Hall's music have also been presented by New York's Casement Fund Song Series in 2016, Princeton's Contemporary Undercurrent of Song Project in 2017, and London's "re-Sung" art song series in 2018. Hall is a Guggenheim Fellow (1989) with a Master's degree from Yale (1987), and her art songs are published by E. C. Schirmer and Boosey & Hawkes.

# Gordon Kerry (APRA)

**b. 1961**

gordonkerry@iinet.net.au
gordonkerry.wordpress.com

Gordon Kerry lives on a hill in Victoria, Australia. Recent works include his *Third Piano Trio*, *Fifth String Quartet*, his fourth opera, *The Snow Queen* (with John Kinsella, for Victorian Opera), his *Second String Quintet*, for the Australian String Quartet and Pieter Wispelwey, and *Victorian Pastoral* for the Young Voices of Melbourne and Ensemble Liaison.

Other recent works include song-cycles on poetry by David Malouf (for mezzo) and Jean Cocteau (for baritone); the opera *Snow White and Other Grimm Tales* (also with John Kinsella); a violin concerto, *So Dream thy Sails* and chamber works for ensemble in Australia, the UK and Europe.

Other vocal music includes the orchestral song cycle for soprano, *Kindled Skies*; the operas *Midnight Son* and *Medea* (which had its US debut at the Kennedy Center in 1994); choral works such as *For those in peril on the sea* for youth choirs and orchestra, *Through the Fire* for soprano, tenor choir and orchestra, and a completion of the Mozart *Requiem* commissioned by the Australian Broadcasting Commission for the 2006 celebrations, as well as a cappella pieces for concert and liturgical use.

He is the author of *New Classical Music: Composing Australia* and other publications and studied at the University of Melbourne with Barry Conyngham.

# Joshua Lindsay

**b. 1988**

joshua.alan.lindsay@gmail.com
www.joshuaalanlindsay.com

Baritone and composer Joshua Alan Lindsay is a native of Nashville, TN. He received his bachelors degree in composition and his masters degree in vocal performance from Austin Peay State University, where he studied under Jeffrey Wood. During his college coursework, he also benefitted from one-on-one lessons with composers-in-residence Lee Hoiby, Chen Yi, Sydney Guillaume, and Anthony Plog, among others. His compositional output consists chiefly of art song setting both pre-existing and original texts.

He works primarily as a vocalist and is currently making his way down the long, arduous road to becoming a professional opera singer. He most recently played the role of Judge Turpin in Sweeney Todd as part of the Hawaii Performing Arts Festival's 2018 season. Recent opera credits include the Bonze in Madama Butterfly, Escamillo in Carmen, Sir Marmaduke Pointdextre in Gilbert and Sullivan's The Sorcerer, the dual roles of Keith and the Father in Lee Hoiby's This is the Rill Speaking, and Tobia Mill in Rossini's La cambiale di matrimonio. As an advocate for new music, Lindsay happily lends his voice to other composers to help premiere their works.

# Cecilia Livingston (ASCAP/SOCAN)

**b. 1984**

cecilia.livingston@gmail.com
www.cecilialivingston.com

With music described as "haunting" and "eerily beautiful" (Tapestry Opera), British-Canadian composer Cecilia Livingston specializes in music for voice. She is a Social Sciences and Humanities Research Council of Canada Postdoctoral Fellow in Music at King's College London, and for 2019-2021 she will be embedded at Glyndebourne through their "Balancing the Score" emerging composer development program. She was a 2015-2017 Composition Fellow at American Opera Projects in New York. Her music has been performed by the Toronto Symphony Orchestra, at Nuit Blanche, and at Bang on a Can's summer festival. Winner of the Canadian Music Centre's 2018 Toronto Emerging Composer Award and the Mécénat Musica Prix 3 Femmes for female opera creators, she is working on Terror & Erebus, a chamber opera for TorQ Percussion Quartet and Opera 5. She has published in The Opera Quarterly, Cambridge Opera Journal, and Tempo, and has presented papers on contemporary opera at the Royal Musical Association and American Musicological Society annual conferences.

An associate composer of the Canadian Music Centre and a National Councilor of the Canadian League of Composers, her creative and research work is supported by the Canada Council for the Arts, the Ontario Arts Council, the Toronto Arts Council, the SOCAN Foundation, and the Social Sciences and Humanities Research Council of Canada. She holds a doctorate in Composition from the University of Toronto, where she was awarded the Theodoros Mirkopoulos Fellowship in Composition.

# Ray Lustig (ASCAP)

rlustig@juilliard.edu
www.raymondlustig.com

Composer Raymond J. Lustig's ever-evolving work ranges from symphonic, to chamber, technological, multimedia, and lately, theatrical. Commissions, performances, and support have come from the Bartok Plusz Opera Festival, Budpaest Operetta Theater, Grand Rapids Symphony, American Composers Orchestra, Town Hall Seattle, the Academy, Metropolis Ensemble, Copland House, American Opera Projects, the Alfred P. Sloan Foundation, New York State Council on the Arts, New York City Ballet's Choreographic Institute, the Norfolk Festival, the St. Louis Guitar Festival, New York Festival of Song, the Caramoor Music Festival, and numerous others. He has served as composer in residence with the Chamber Music Festival of Lexington, the Imagine Science Film Festival, and Copland House's Compose Yourself project. Lustig's awards include the Charles Ives Fellowship from the American Academy of Arts and Letters, ASCAP's Rudolf Nissim Prize for his orchestral work UNSTUCK, and the Aaron Copland Award from Copland House. His teachers have included John Corigliano, Robert Beaser, Samuel Adler, Sebastian Currier, Jonathan Kramer, Derek Bermel, Philip Lasser, Pia Gilbert, and Conrad Cummings.

# Carrie Magin (ASCAP)

b. 1981

www.carriemagin.com

With music of luminous vocal resonance, percussive intensity, and shimmering instrumentation, internationally-performed composer Carrie Magin traverses a wide emotional range with her fresh and universal voice.

Her current interests revolve around the relationship between text (sung or spoken) and music, with commissions by Georgia College Choral Ensembles, University of Cincinnati CCM Chorale, UC Women's Chorus, The Cincinnati Review, bass trombonist Russ Zokaites, and the Immanuel Presbyterian Choir in Cincinnati, OH. Recent performances include the premiere of her choral work "Heart-Fire" in Carnegie Hall in 2018 and the performance of her mini-opera "Voice on the Wire" by Boston Opera Collaborative in 2017.

Additional honors include a Fulbright Teaching Assistantship, two Art Education Grants from the New York State Council on the Arts, a Strategic Opportunity Stipend from the New York Foundation for the Arts, and composer residencies with Georgia Institute of Technology, Minnesota State University Moorhead, and Chamber Music Campania in Foggia, Italy.

Carrie Magin holds degrees from the University of Michigan and the University of Cincinnati College-Conservatory of Music. She is a member of the composition faculty at Interlochen Arts Camp, and she is currently Assistant Professor of Composition and Theory at Houghton College, where she was nominated for the Excellence in Teaching Award in 2017.

# James Matheson (ASCAP)

b. 1970

www.jamesmatheson.com

New York-based composer James Matheson is widely regarded as one of the most distinctive, vital, and creative musical voices of his generation. Among his commissions are works for the New York and Los Angeles Philharmonics, the Chicago and Albany Symphony Orchestras, Carnegie Hall, and the St. Lawrence and Borromeo String Quartets. The American Academy of Arts and Letters honored him in December, 2011 with the Charles Ives Living.

Recent commissions include a new work for large orchestra, commissioned by the Los Angeles Philharmonic, to be premiered February 24th, 25th and 26th, 2017; *Violin Concerto*, co-commissioned by the Chicago Symphony Orchestra and the Los Angeles Philharmonic; *True South*, commissioned by the New York Philharmonic; *The Age of Air*, for two shakuhachi and chamber orchestra, co-commissioned by Kyo-Shin-An Arts and River Oaks Chamber Orchestra for soloists James Schlefer and Akihito Obama; *String Quartet* (2014), commissioned by Justus and Elizabeth Schlichting for the St. Lawrence String Quartet; *Times Alone* (2013), commissioned by soprano Kiera Duffy, *Cretic Variations* (2013), commissioned by pianist Nadia Shpachenko, and *Peace Talks* (2014), commissioned by Swarthmore College for its Sesquicentennial Celebration. Other recent projects include new works for violinist Jennifer Koh, pianist Bruce Levingston and pianist Nadia Schpachenko.

From 2009 to 2015 James served as Director of the the Los Angeles Philharmonic's innovative Composer Fellowship Program. In addition to the Ives Living award, Matheson has received fellowships and awards from the Guggenheim Foundation, Civitella Ranieri, the Bogliasco and Sage Foundations, ASCAP, and the Robbins Prize. From 2005-2007, Matheson was Executive Director of the MATA Festival of New Music in New York, which commissions and performs the work of young composers who are making their entry into professional musical life. Matheson has held residencies at Yaddo and the Liguria Study Center, and has been a fellow at the Aspen Music Festival and the Norfolk Chamber Music Festival.

# James Primosch (BMI)

b. 1956

www.jamesprimosch.com

When honoring him with its Goddard Lieberson Fellowship, the American Academy of Arts and Letters noted that "A rare economy of means and a strain of religious mysticism distinguish the music of James Primosch… Through articulate, transparent textures, he creates a wide range of musical emotion." Andrew Porter stated in *The New Yorker* that Primosch "scores with a sure, light hand" and critics for the *New York Times*, the *Chicago Sun-Times*, the *Philadelphia Inquirer*, and the *Dallas Morning News* have characterized his music as "impressive", "striking", "grandly romantic", "stunning" and "very approachable".

Primosch's compositional voice encompasses a broad range of expressive types. His music can be intensely lyrical, as in the song cycle *Holy the Firm* (composed for Dawn Upshaw) or dazzlingly angular as in *Secret Geometry* for piano and electronic sound. His affection for jazz is reflected in works like the *Piano Quintet*, while his work as a church musician informs the many pieces in his catalog based on sacred songs or religious texts.

Born in Cleveland, Ohio in 1956, James Primosch studied at Cleveland State University, the University of Pennsylvania, and Columbia University. He counts Mario Davidovsky, George Crumb and Richard Wernick among his principal teachers.

James Primosch is also active as a pianist, particularly in the realm of contemporary music. He was a prizewinner at the Gaudeamus Interpreters Competition in Rotterdam, and appears on recordings for New World, CRI, the Smithsonian Collection, and Crystal Records. He has worked as a jazz pianist and a liturgical musician.

Since 1988 he has served on the faculty of the University of Pennsylvania, where he directs the Presser Electronic Music Studio.

# Behzad Ranjbaran (ASCAP)

b. 1955

www.behzadranjbaran.com

Behzad Ranjbaran is known for music which is both evocative and colorful, and also strong in structural integrity and form. He frequently draws inspiration from his cultural roots and Persian heritage in form or subject matter, as exemplified by the tone poems of the "Persian Trilogy", or the interpretation of sounds and styles in works such as the Violin Concerto and Songs of Eternity.

The texts for two choral works also draw directly on Persian culture, as do some of his many chamber works, including *Fountains of Fin*, a eulogy for Amir Kabir, the 19th century slain Iranian vezir; *Shiraz and Isfahan*, celebrating two of Mr. Ranjbaran's favorite cities in Iran; and *Enchanted Garden*, inspired by the many beautiful gardens of his native land.

Described as "music's magical realist" (*Philadelphia Inquirer*) and "a master of the orchestra" (*Dallas Morning News*), Mr. Ranjbaran's compositions possess "radiant luminescence" (*Washington Post*) and "qualities of inherent beauty and strong musical structure that make…a satisfying musical entity" (*Nashville Scene*).

Born on July 1, 1955 in Tehran, Iran, Mr. Ranjbaran is the recipient of the Rudolf Nissim Award for his Violin Concerto. His musical education started early when he entered the Tehran Music Conservatory at the age of nine. He came to the United States in 1974 to attend Indiana University and received his doctorate in composition from The Juilliard School, where he currently serves on the faculty.

# William Toutant (BMI)

**b. 1948**

william.toutant@csun.edu
williamtoutant.weebly.com

William Toutant was born in Worcester, Massachusetts. He received his BA and MA from The George Washington University and his Ph.D. in music theory and composition from Michigan State University. He joined the music faculty of California State University, Northridge in 1975. During the next 38 years he not only taught in the Department of Music, but he also served in a variety of administrative positions including Dean of the Mike Curb College of Arts, Media, and Communication.

For eighteen years, he wrote and hosted the weekly radio program, "The KCSN Opera House." He became Professor Emeritus in May 2013. His music is available on North/South, Capstone, Centaur, Phasma and Navona records.

He lives in Los Angeles with his wife, Ligia Toutant.

# Theodore Wiprud (ASCAP)

b. 1958

www.theodorewiprud.com

Theodore Wiprud is a composer, educator, and arts leader. He is widely known for having served as Vice President, Education, at the New York Philharmonic from 2004-2018, and as host of the iconic Young People's Concerts.

At the same time, he has produced a steady stream of works including a *Sinfonietta* (2016), premiered by the South Dakota Symphony; a Violin Concerto (*Katrina*), composed for Ittai Shapira, and released with the Royal Liverpool Philharmonic on Champs Hill Records; a one-act opera, *My Last Duchess*, with libretto by Tom Dulack based on poetry by Robert Browning; a song cycle, *For Allegra*, on a variety of American poets; and a number of pieces based on *gugak*, Korean traditional music, and including *gugak* instruments like p'iri, gayageum, and haegeum.

Many of Wiprud's works explore spiritual experience, like the orchestral *Hosannas of the Second Heaven* and *Grail*; his two string quartets; and a number of choral pieces. Other works respond to American literature, including *American Journal*, based on Robert Hayden's poem, and *A Georgia Song*, a setting of Maya Angelou.

Wiprud graduated *cum laude* in biochemistry at Harvard and earned a master's in theory and composition at Boston University, where he worked with David Del Tredici. He also studied with Robin Holloway at Cambridge University, and with Jacob Druckman and Bernard Rands at Aspen.

# Supplementary Materials

Texts, program notes, composer biographies, and composer headshots can be found at:

https://newmusicshelf.com/anthologies/soprano-v1-info/

www.ingramcontent.com/pod-product-compliance
Lightning Source LLC
Chambersburg PA
CBHW080338170426
43194CB00014B/2607